ROCK
YOUR ROLE
AS A
SALESFORCE
ADMIN

CREATE VALUE, CALM THE CHAOS, AND SUPERCHARGE YOUR SALESFORCE CAREER

D1558218

JODI HRBEK

Print ISBN: 978-1-7356702-2-5

eBook ISBN: 978-1-7356702-3-2

 HERBIVORE PRESS

For inquiries: Howdy@HerbivorePress.com

TABLE OF CONTENTS

INTRODUCTION

"Would you like fries with that?"

If you're like most Salesforce admins, you wear a lot of hats. Most of us can be described as a Jack or Jill of all trades. A Renaissance man or woman. A mash-up of technologist, data nerd, business analyst, trainer, traffic cop, change agent, help desk, and herder of cats. Odds are that you love your profession. Still, you've likely had plenty of days when you may have felt like this retort was the best you could offer in response to a constant stream of work coming at you as if you were working the drive-through at McAdmin's. And if you are a seasoned Salesforce admin, you can probably attest that the more value you deliver, the faster and more furiously the demands and competing projects seem to come.

Once an "accidental" career that people fell into as they were tasked with maintaining the Salesforce application in addition to doing their day job, the Salesforce admin role has morphed into a sought-after and lucrative career choice. As companies running businesses on the Salesforce platform proliferate, the Salesforce admin role is in such demand that staffing firms are recruiting candidates for free training programs to cultivate enough talent to meet their clients' needs.

According to the Salesforce website, the average salary for a Salesforce admin is $91,000, and there is a 400 percent annual growth rate in new jobs.[1] Experienced Salesforce admins can command even higher wages and have the luxury of choosing their work environment and the specific type of work they want. If you're a seasoned Salesforce admin with a rockstar reputation, you can write your own ticket. And you can rest easy knowing that you can make a living in even the most challenging job market.

Great pay. Job security. Dynamic work. And you get to spend your days solving problems, improving efficiency, and making a noticeable contribution to your company. The Salesforce admin role is one of the absolute best jobs, and those who get to do it for a living are a fortunate bunch!

It's not easy, though. It takes hard work to become a Salesforce admin. It takes additional effort and an entirely different set of skills to transform yourself from an order taker to a value-add partner in your organization. Successful Salesforce admins need to extract the *real* problem statement instead of jumping to execute a requested solution. You must prioritize and execute tactical work and projects requiring concentration and deep thought while dealing with continual interruptions and changing priorities. You need to diplomatically manage the chaos to get things across the finish line, which requires navigating trade-offs, pushing back on unreasonable requests, and having the business savvy to do these things without alienating users or infuriating stakeholders. These abilities don't come easily to most people and may be particularly challenging for people attracted to this work, who love to say yes and solve problems. If you can master these skills, coupled with your Salesforce admin superpowers, the payoff can be tremendous.

The conundrum for many Salesforce admins is that the more successful they are at solving their organization's problems, the more their company's Salesforce footprint expands. Marketing wants in. The Proposal team wants in. The Delivery team sees the benefit of the process automation, and now they want in. Finance wants to start leveraging the data and reporting and requires a dashboard of its own. Customer Service sees what's going on and wants in, too.

Unfortunately, expansion often comes without a proportionate increase in Salesforce resources when companies fail to account for the maintenance of all this new functionality in their future-year budgets. Even if your scope is limited to working with one business team, the more great solutions you deliver, the more in demand you become. You suddenly have more users with questions, more functionality to maintain, more reports to tweak, more data to monitor, more changes to implement, and more people who want a piece of you. Sound familiar? Being in high demand because you've made a measurable impact and earned a reputation as a problem solver within your organization is an excellent place to be, but it can wear you down.

Does this mean you should stop delivering great work or that this was the wrong career choice? Of course not. We've established that you've got one of the best jobs out there. Excelling in this role will pay off in spades over time with opportunities—financial and otherwise—that will be afforded to you. However, long-term success is a two-way street. A satisfying, sustainable Salesforce career requires not only that you create value for your stakeholders but that you are equally intentional in establishing rules of engagement and business boundaries that work for you. If you've landed a gig as a Salesforce admin, you've already proven that you've got impressive chops. Your Salesforce skills are your ticket to ride. Where you go on your career journey will be directly tied to the value you provide and how you interact with your colleagues and constituents, including setting expectations for how they should interact with you.

Who Is the Intended Audience for this Book?

I wrote this book for Salesforce professionals with some or all of the responsibility for managing the Salesforce application within their organization. Your title may be sys admin, business analyst, system analyst, sales ops, rev ops, Salesforce guru, CRM manager, or anything in between. Regardless of what you're called, you're responsible for maintaining and enhancing the Salesforce application.

Based on how Salesforce is used and supported at your company, you may report to the sales organization, technology team, call center, or, if you work for a nonprofit, the fundraising director. You may be what we refer to as a solo admin, with responsibility for all facets of the system, or you may work in an enterprise organization where you're part of a large Salesforce team and have a more narrow focus. If you spend some of your time interacting with users and stakeholders, some of your time using tools such as Report Builder and Data Loader, and much of your time deep in the weeds in Salesforce Setup, building great Salesforce solutions, this book is for you.

If you're a freshly minted, certified Salesforce admin or relatively new to the Salesforce world, welcome aboard! While this book assumes that you understand the terminology and basics of Salesforce administration, you don't have to be an expert. I'll cover the nontechnical aspects of the role and provide field-tested strategies to set you up for success and shorten your learning curve on the people and process parts of being a Salesforce admin.

If you're a more seasoned Salesforce admin, perhaps already sporting multiple credentials and connected to the Salesforce Ohana, this book is for you, too. Most Salesforce admins I know love what they do but are extremely busy and feel overwhelmed by the spinning plates, demanding stakeholders, and long days. You may already be making a Salesforce rockstar salary, but if you consider that along with the long hours you work, you may find your situation not so stellar. If this sounds familiar and you'd like to add some tools to your arsenal to help you calm the chaos, this book is for you.

What This Book Doesn't Cover

I don't provide an overview of Salesforce platform capabilities or detail the differences between Sales Cloud, Service Cloud, and Marketing Cloud. You won't find instructions on setting up roles, profiles, revenue schedules, or any other Salesforce functionality. If you picked up this book to prepare for a certification, learn Flow Builder, learn how to write complex formulas, or get tips on creating dynamic Lightning pages, you won't find that here. I reference Salesforce functionality throughout the book in the context of examining solutioning requests from business stakeholders and leveraging system capabilities to provide value, but there are no technical "how-to" instructions or hands-on-keyboard exercises.

It's not that these topics aren't critical for the Salesforce admin; it's simply that plenty of material is already available on the fundamentals of the Salesforce platform and the declarative skills required to become a Salesforce certified administrator. There are great books and blogs. There is Trailhead, the free learning site published by Salesforce. You can Google any question about Salesforce and find dozens of community pages, videos, and recorded Dreamforce (the annual user conference) sessions.

Maybe you're wondering: "What? A Salesforce book that doesn't tell you how to do Salesforce? What's left to cover?"

Extraordinary Salesforce admins create tremendous value and deserve a role that leaves them feeling energized, not overly taxed. So this book will help you position yourself as a Salesforce superhero in your company and arm you with tools and techniques to create business boundaries and a sustainable workload.

The content is organized in two parts, each with short chapters packed with actionable advice. You'll find field-tested pro tips, real-life examples, and lists of dos and don'ts. These bite-sized suggestions can help you immediately implement new strategies and ideas.

Part 1: Create Value and a Raving Fan Base

There are baseline expectations for any Salesforce admin. You must be proficient, productive, and professional. And you must know a heck of a lot about how Salesforce works—the core competencies. To flourish in the role and earn the respect of your constituents as a value-adding business partner with the domain authority and fan base to prove it, there's much more to the story. Yes, of course you need to add users, terminate them when they leave, answer questions, tweak functionality, and run requested reports, but that's not what will get you recognized and rewarded. The first part of this book provides practical suggestions and techniques to create value for your stakeholders. I share tactics for establishing your domain authority as a Salesforce admin pro and your reputation as a trusted advisor instead of being relegated to an order taker. I provide real-world scenarios and sample talk tracks so you can see how these skills are applied and hear how certain conversations might sound.

In the first part of the book, you will:

- Understand the reasons it's worth your time and energy to go above and beyond, and how this will benefit your career and earnings well beyond your current position

- Learn the Salesforce admin pro competencies that will establish your domain authority and differentiate you as an indispensable resource

- Discover how you can use questions to uncover business outcomes and identify the right solution

- Get tips for gaining influence and improving your communication with key business stakeholders

Part 2: Calm the Chaos

Even if they have the best intentions, your stakeholders ask a lot of you. We Salesforce admins love to over deliver, sometimes to our own detriment.

What if you could partner with your stakeholders to create a timeline based on the complexity of the ask and the reality of your workload instead of jumping into a task the minute someone needs something ASAP? What if, instead of being on the order-taking end at McAdmin's Drive-Thru, you could set the pace for deployments and iterative releases? Instead of saying yes when you're already overwhelmed, what if you could propose mutually beneficial trade-offs that result in reduced scope or additional time and resources to create a win-win for you *and* them?

The second part of this book provides actionable processes and techniques. If you're going to over deliver, go above and beyond, and wow your constituents, you must be armed accordingly. You'll learn how to establish rules of engagement that will get you out of order-taker mode and allow you to work using a more consultative, measured approach. I'll give you creative ways to push back and leave your constituents smiling even when you have to tell them no.

In the second part of the book, you will:

- Hear about processes you can implement to organize your work and add structure to your stakeholder interactions

- Learn techniques for establishing more-realistic timelines and reducing the need for personal heroics

- Consider what things you might stop doing to reduce your overwhelm

- Understand why Salesforce admins are at risk of burning out, and learn a few things you can do to prevent that

As with Salesforce solutions, there's no one-size-fits-all approach for Salesforce admin success. Depending on how your specific role is structured, how your company operates, and what's going down on any given day, some of these strategies may work for you and some may not be applicable. You may be in a role where you can influence which Salesforce solutions are delivered and what processes are in place, or you may have limited say in these matters. Either way, you can practice the core skills, consider the central boundary-setting principles, and recommend process improvements as applicable.

Some of this advice may seem contrarian. Say no? Deliver something different than what was requested? Give your business stakeholders action items? It won't all be appropriate in all situations. However, these are field-tested techniques to make you indispensable within your organization while maintaining a semblance of control over the things coming at you. I'm confident that if you try even a tenth of what's here, you'll enjoy some immediate benefits.

Use this book as a reference guide. Read through the chapter headings and see what resonates. Try a few things out and see what works. Then revisit it as needed.

Why Am I Qualified to Write this Book?

Simply put, I've "been there, done that" as far as being a Salesforce admin is concerned. I've successfully done Salesforce for a living in some way, shape, or form for two decades. I completed my first small Salesforce implementation in 2001. I deployed Salesforce for 300 users a year later at the global consulting firm where I spearheaded business development initiatives. Many Salesforce customers now have multiple thousands of users, but a deployment that size was significant back then.

My company was one of the first to run Enterprise Edition, the license level that had just been introduced. We had such great success implementing our CRM that we stood up a separate org to manage our recruiting process. This use case was quite progressive then, resulting in requests to demo it for Salesforce's up-and-coming recruiting team, who eventually recruited me.

I attended the first Dreamforce, where I vividly recall meeting with a product manager to explain why we so desperately needed the ability to use "or" as a report filter. Believe it or not, back then, if someone needed to see this *or* that in a report, we had to provide two different reports.

Around that time, I hosted the first Dallas user group meeting at my office. I presented on the topic of data quality at the second Dreamforce, well before duplicate rules and fuzzy matching. When I started my Salesforce career, it was before Apex, before Visualforce, and before there was an option to purchase a sandbox, so we made changes directly in our production environment. Yikes!

I worked directly for Salesforce for four years as an account executive and a customer success manager, providing best practices around adoption, data management, and governance for some of the largest enterprise accounts. While there, I previewed the AppExchange to customers and prospects at regional events and city tours before it was even a "thing."

After that, I was the sole implementer and admin responsible for dozens of deployments during the years I hung out my shingle as a freelance consultant.

In director and VP roles, when I managed the Salesforce platform for several enterprise companies, I led teams comprised of both Salesforce admins and developers on complex deployments. I've worked with start-ups, small companies, non-profits, and publicly traded organizations, sometimes as an employee, sometimes as a consultant, and sometimes as a volunteer. I've deployed and managed traditional Sales Cloud and Service Cloud implementations and led a team that built a custom platform-as-a-service (PaaS) org used by every employee in the company.

I have directly hired and managed more than 25 Salesforce admins, assembling some of the best teams in the business. I have trained and coached dozens more through my consulting gigs and tenure at Salesforce. I have a broad perspective to share on this topic, as I've seen the gamut, from Salesforce admins who rocked it, to some who needed a little coaching and eventually got there, to a handful who either couldn't or wouldn't succeed, so I helped them find a better fit. I've been doing this long enough to have witnessed many newbie Salesforce admins grow into seasoned architects and consulting professionals. Many of my former team members, including several I hired right out of college and former clients I trained on the Salesforce platform, now earn big bucks and have fancy titles across various roles in the Salesforce ecosystem.

I'm fortunate that I've not only had a broad range of experience but that my success has given me the luxury to pick and choose the gigs I take, set an aggressive pay rate, and do it all from the comfort of my home office in the Texas Hill Country, with zero commute and my pack of rescue dogs at my feet. I haven't actively looked for a job or had to hustle for clients in years, as I've maintained a steady backlog of former employers, colleagues, and clients with long project lists. I'm sharing this not to brag but to drive home the benefits of racking up a solid Salesforce track record.

I feel very fortunate, as my Salesforce career has served me well both personally and professionally. Yet, candidly, I've worked more hours over the years than I care to admit, and on far too many occasions, I've watched my team perform personal heroics to keep up with stakeholder demands.

Why Is this Book Valuable?

The idea for this book surfaced as a debrief exercise. Several years ago, on the brink of burnout, I quit my job as VP of sales technology at a large IT services company. In addition to overseeing all things on the Salesforce platform, my small but mighty team of Salesforce admins had recently completed an enormous initiative to decommission a legacy system using far fewer resources than the project warranted. I was physically and mentally exhausted but still wanted to capture all the things that had worked well. Even more critical, I wanted to apply hindsight to the things I could have implemented or stopped doing that would have helped my team work smarter.

In my next role, I applied these insights and continued to identify and refine techniques and processes to calm the chaos amid a demanding delivery schedule.

As I started thinking through what I wanted to share in this book, I realized that many of the conversations I now have with current and former teammates have little to do with Salesforce functionality. Instead, they're focused on topics such as managing relationships with stakeholders and navigating unrealistic expectations from the business. And there are inevitably requests for career advice.

My lengthy tenure in the Salesforce space has given me a unique vantage point. Sure, I can talk about how to help companies fully leverage their Salesforce investment, and I can help Salesforce admins avoid a few platform gotchas. More importantly, I can discuss the value-adding approaches that have worked wonders for my Salesforce admin teams and me. I can also share cautionary tales about overwork and burnout. I feel passionately that any book about going above and beyond must have an equal focus on techniques to prevent this.

The Salesforce platform has expanded tremendously in the past 20 years. Opportunities for Salesforce admins have grown exponentially, as have both the complexity of and expectations for the role. My goal is to shorten your learning curve by sharing what I've learned—sometimes the hard way—throughout my journey. Mostly, I hope to help you leverage your hard-earned Salesforce skills in a manner that energizes you, allows you to deliver great Salesforce solutions, and gives you the satisfying and rewarding career you deserve.

Let's do this!

QUICK NOTE ON TERMINOLOGY

Throughout this book, I use a few terms I'd like to call out to ensure that we're on the same page.

Constituents refers to all of your internal customers. These may include but are not limited to company executives, business process owners, consumers of the data, and the teams that use the system. Many technology teams refer to their business stakeholders as "the business" as if they're part of a separate entity. If you work for the same team and share the same overall objectives, you are part of the business, so I prefer the term "business partner" to reflect this. I refer to constituents interchangeably as business partners, stakeholders, and, more informally, your peeps.

Business as usual (BAU) refers to the things you do regularly to keep the lights on—the daily actions required to maintain the status quo, support users, troubleshoot existing functionality, and make sure Salesforce works as expected. BAU also includes the small changes and bite-sized system enhancements that are standard fare for most Salesforce admins.

Projects and initiatives involve deploying new functionality or making significant system enhancements. They may be large projects organized by your company's centralized project management office (PMO) or larger initiatives you're working on with a business unit to add functionality or support new business processes. These are value-adding things that move the needle for stakeholders but that you must balance against the demands of BAU activity.

Your queue refers to the collective body of tickets, tasks, and enhancement requests you're responsible for across your BAU and project work, regardless of the system you use to manage and prioritize your work. (Don't worry if you haven't systemized this yet, we'll cover it in part two.)

PART 1

CREATE VALUE
AND A RAVING FAN BASE

CHAPTER 1

HAVE AN OWNERSHIP MINDSET

Take stands, take risks, take responsibility.

—Muriel Siebert

A few years ago, I was approached by a company looking for someone to lead its Salesforce initiatives. While meeting with my potential new boss at a coffee shop, he asked, "Who tells you what to do every day?" At the time, I reported to the SVP of sales, who had no clue about the care and feeding of Salesforce. He didn't need to know. He'd hired me because he needed an accurate forecast, a full pipeline, and a way to manage what the reps were or were not doing.

After a pause, I explained that I listened to my stakeholders' needs, regularly sat with my users, and paid attention to my company's top-level objectives. At the same time, I was focused on ensuring that my system was secure, had clean data, had no defunct infrastructure, and was leveraging the latest and greatest functionality. That, I explained, was how I determined what needed to be done each day, adding that I occasionally consulted with my boss to prioritize based on his knowledge of critical initiatives.

I could sense his confusion. He then asked, "If your boss doesn't tell you what to do, how does he know you're doing any work?"

I immediately knew I didn't want this person as my next boss. If he felt the need to ask me that question, he and I were not aligned in our work philosophies. "Takes one to know one," I thought, imagining this dude with his feet on his desk, doing as much of nothing as he could get away with when his boss wasn't looking.

I no longer recall how I answered that question. In hindsight, I imagine a movie moment where I stand on my chair in that coffee shop. Cue the dramatic orchestra music. With my fist in the air, or perhaps waving a Trailblazer hoodie, I give an indignant speech on behalf of all hard-working, self-respecting Salesforce admins:

How does he know I'm doing work? Well, sir, when you do it right, you create a fan club. Not just ordinary fans, but raving ones. The kind that call your boss to tell them what a great job you're doing. The ones who stand up at a sales meeting and say they would be remiss in not mentioning that they were able to re-capture so much lost business because the Salesforce team helped put together an awesome campaign to identify and target deals lost in the last 18 months. The ones who brag to the CEO about the incredible case routing and Live Agent support implemented in record time.

It is my system. It is my responsibility to make it work, to keep it secure, and to consider how to make it easier to use for all my peeps who log in every day. I wake up in the middle of the night with ideas about how to make it better. And guess what, it does *keep getting better every day.* That *is how my boss knows!*

An Ownership Mindset

When I recounted this story to a friend, melodrama and all, she suggested that the question fired me up so much because I have an ownership mindset. Her comment and some research on the topic helped me recognize that this mentality is undoubtedly a trait that differentiates the rockstar Salesforce admins I've met over the years from those who were just okay.

In the Salesforce admin role, an ownership mindset means holding yourself accountable for the success and quality of the Salesforce platform.

An article about ownership mindset in *Inc.* summed this up perfectly. "It's the difference between those who achieve and those who stumble, those who rise up and those who get left behind." The author compiled a list of fundamental principles of this mindset: accepting personal responsibility, finding creative ways through obstacles, keeping the mission always in mind, taking extra initiative, and maintaining "a burning urgency to do more, accomplish more, grow more, and learn more."[2]

It's important to note that having an ownership mindset has nothing to do with your title or rank. It's an attitude and an approach. It means you are willing to lead and innovate instead of accepting the status quo.

As Salesforce professionals, we are caretakers of a critical application that can impact the company's top and bottom line. It directly affects how associates do their work every day and their level of engagement. As they say, with great power comes great responsibility. In exchange for this and the corresponding paycheck that we already established is not so shabby, Salesforce admins with an ownership mindset strive not just to keep the lights on but to truly add value and give people more than they expect or more than they know to ask for.

To add value is to bring your perspective and expertise to the table. It means paying attention to the small details while considering the big-picture implications. It means going above and beyond and overdelivering. The value you bring to the role every day is what lets you ultimately create a crowd of colleagues who will swear that you are indispensable.

Throughout my career, I've encountered some Salesforce admins who were content to be ordinary or "phone it in." To my astonishment, on one consulting engagement, I met a woman who had been the sole Salesforce admin at her company for almost a decade, yet she had never built a single dashboard! As I walked her through the basics of dashboard creation, generally one of the more entry-level Salesforce admin tasks, I asked how it was possible she'd never done it before. She shrugged and said, "No one ever asked for one." Definitely no ownership mindset there.

I've also met many Salesforce admins new to the role who eagerly approach their job with the desire to wow their stakeholders but aren't sure how to translate that beyond the clear-cut support facets of their position. I believe many people would love to exhibit their ownership mindset but may be relatively green in their career or new in the Salesforce admin role and unsure of exactly what to do or how to do it beyond what's obvious. That's a big reason I wrote this book: to specify what adding value looks like for a Salesforce admin.

What's in It for You?

Before we dive into these next chapters, you may wonder if all this value-creation stuff is really necessary. "If I'm already doing an okay job, why shake up the status quo?" You may be asking, "Adding value and having an ownership mindset sounds like extra work, and I'm already slammed. What's in it for me?"

I get it! It's hard to learn Salesforce, keep up with all the new releases, and get through your daily responsibilities, but it is a worthwhile investment to go the extra mile. If you are on the fence about putting in the extra effort, here are four reasons to stick with it.

- **To stand out.** First there's a pragmatic reason. Salesforce admin skills are in high demand and will undoubtedly continue to be for the foreseeable future, but the number of certified Salesforce admins is increasing rapidly. Salesforce provides free training. Recruiting firms are offering free training to grow a candidate base. More and more people are displaying Salesforce certifications on their LinkedIn profiles. To stand out as a superstar, you'll need to do more than simply know your way around the Setup menu.

- **To progress your career.** The steps you take to stand out and be indispensable will allow you to fully monetize your hard-earned Salesforce admin skills and better control how you apply and grow those skills. That might mean your company throws money at you with big, fat annual raises and funding for your trip to Dreamforce every year. Depending on your career plans, it might mean moving from a hands-on-keyboard job to one where you ultimately oversee the Salesforce program. Or it could mean you get more say in work assigned to you, ensuring that you get the plum gigs and an opportunity to delegate the more rote tasks required to manage the system. Having a vocal fan base and a reputation as indispensable gets you on the promotion fast track and ultimately allows you to command above-market wages.

- **To establish a rockstar reputation.** The value you deliver earns you domain authority and gives you the street cred to push back on your stakeholders when needed. It's what enables you to set ground rules and engage on your terms. Your track record of success, coupled with your fan base, is what ultimately shapes your personal brand. It's the currency you'll use to get recognized and rewarded in your current role and to empower you on whatever future Salesforce journey you envision.

- **To love your work.** Let's face it, it feels amazing to deliver great solutions and earn rave reviews.

What if you could incorporate a few new tactics to ensure that you are a person your colleagues will remember years after you leave because you made such a significant impact? What if doing a few different things, adjusting a few current behaviors, or learning a few new tricks could make you the kind of employee your company desperately wants to retain, promote, and continue to develop? What if your domain knowledge and track record of success could let you reframe business requests in a way that enables you to deliver what you know they need, not just what they asked for?

If that all sounds worthwhile, let's roll up our sleeves and explore precisely what successful value-adding Salesforce admins do to accomplish this.

CHAPTER 2:

TABLE STAKES: KNOW THY COMPANY, THY PEEPS, AND THY ORG

Most of all, I discovered that in order to succeed with a product
you must truly get to know your customer
and build something for them.

—Marc Benioff

We've established that you need to know a great deal of information about the Salesforce platform. This is just the tip of the iceberg if you plan to make a lasting impression as a Salesforce admin extraordinaire. As with the stakes in any casino game, there's a minimum you've got to bring to the table. You must take the time to understand your company's critical business drivers, not to mention details such as the organization's vernacular and meeting cadence. You must know the central objectives for the teams that use Salesforce and be intimately familiar with their business processes and how they work in the system. And, of course, you must know the intricate details of the system itself.

As we dive into specific ways Salesforce admins can earn domain authority and a raving fan base, all the strategies presume that you possess this baseline knowledge. The items I cover in this chapter are the prerequisites or table stakes. Imagine how much more value you can create when you know exactly what problems your constituents are trying to solve at all levels, including macro-level company objectives and tactical things that may be most vexing to your users.

If you've been in your role, or at least employed at your company, for a long time, you've probably already got a handle on the basics. If so, take a quick read to see if any areas require a little brushing up. Perhaps this section will remind you to reach out to certain business sponsors or users you haven't caught up with in a while. It may also prompt you to finally dig into that one mysterious and complicated section of your org that you may be avoiding.

Know thy Company

Have you ever sat in a meeting where an arrogant sales rep was trying to sell you some Salesforce add-on, convinced they knew precisely what would solve your biggest problem? Yet, they never took the time to understand what problem you were trying to solve or even how your company was using Salesforce. I'm sure it was evident to you that they were giving you a canned song and dance instead of caring about the intricacies of your particular pain point.

As in any sales or consulting relationship, the value you can bring is directly proportionate to your knowledge about your company, its mission, and its organizational priorities. Effective collaboration and the ability to solve problems for your stakeholders require an in-depth understanding of their goals and unique business challenges.

Even if you know the company objectives at a high level, you won't have any credibility if you don't speak about them in the language your company uses. Are the people who buy your products or services called clients, customers, or something else? Do you understand your company's value proposition and the specific reasons your customers do business with you?

Get to know your industry, including the main competitors, significant trends, and any nuances relating to the regulatory environment. This is particularly important if you work in healthcare, banking, or another industry with regulations that may impact how you manage specific data types or business processes within the platform.

The aim is to understand how the people and processes you support contribute to the organization's overall success. How do the company goals cascade down to the department level? This will help you identify the areas where you can best add value and make an impact.

You also need to understand the organizational structure and business processes that support it. Where are there points of intersection between teams? What information does the Customer Success team rely on from Sales? How does Sales align with Marketing? Is there a Demand Gen function? How is that team organized? Where's the handoff? How does each team define roles and responsibilities?

You aren't just a Salesforce expert. As a Salesforce admin, you're a vital member of the company's operations, so you must understand how the company operates.

In terms of knowing all the critical facets of your company, you may feel like you have this covered. Excellent! You'll be ready to apply this knowledge in the next section. Otherwise, here are some suggestions:

- Read your company's website and intranet site from top to bottom

- Follow the company on social media

- Set up a Google alert for news mentions

- If the company is public, read the quarterly and annual company reports, review analyst research, and listen to earnings calls. Pay attention to the questions analysts are asking to identify hot topics; see if you can make connections between those issues and the projects on your plate

- Ask your business leads for any key presentations that provide insight into their department's objectives and priorities. Request an invitation to any recurring meetings at which they review operational results

Pro tip: Start a glossary of critical terms for the company or the business unit you work with, including acronyms, to increase your fluency with the vernacular and company-specific business concepts.

Pro tip: Get to know the culture of your company. The tone of user communications, training materials, and even the tenor of error messages in validation rules should reflect your organization's character. If you work for a financial institution, you probably don't want "Hey! What about me?" as the error message when someone leaves a critical field blank. But if you work for a start-up with a casual vibe, injecting some of the company's personality into the system can be a hit.

Know thy Peeps

True confession time. My team and I once spent several hours setting up an approval process, absolutely convinced that it would be a massive win for the management team responsible for doing the approvals. During a conversation about their business challenges, the team leader mentioned that they were experiencing significant delays getting things approved. Approval delays! We knew how to solve those, or so we thought.

We went to work, quite certain that they would benefit from the automatic routing and email reply functionality we could set up in a relative jiffy. As we were preparing to demo what we were sure would knock their socks off, we found out information we should've known all along: these particular managers were behind the wheel almost all day, often with long stretches of driving, so they couldn't regularly keep up with all the approval emails or interact with the app. We were solving the wrong problem, or at the very least, bringing them the wrong solution for the situation because we hadn't invested the time to understand how they worked and what they needed.

This story illustrates several rookie mistakes I cover in upcoming chapters, such as not confirming the problem and not validating assumptions, highlighting a fundamental rule: you must understand how your users work. Literally, where are they when they're working? How do they access information? What type of device are they using? How do they interact with their systems, data, customers, and colleagues? Can you define the use case for each type of user in your system? Have you seen firsthand how they use it?

The practice of watching your users work is so critical to Salesforce admin success that it's earned a name, Salesforce administration by walking around (SABWA). It's a take-off on management by walking around (MBWA), in which managers go into the trenches with their employees to gain personal insight that can't be gleaned from data and reports.

This practice of spending time with users is invaluable. Every time I watch how different team members interact with the system, I learn something I can use to make the system better. If you haven't done this before or if you have, but it's been a while, get this scheduled.

In a perfect world, SABWA entails sitting deskside with your users or even doing a ride-along with a sales rep or field technician. In a world where many people are working remotely, you may need to be creative in conducting virtual sessions, but even so, you can learn a great deal of information that way.

From a Sales Cloud perspective, the purpose is to learn firsthand what your sales reps do to prepare for their meetings and watch how they do (or don't) record their meeting details in Salesforce. If you have an inside sales team, shadow a lead gen specialist. How do they work through their lead list? Which reports or dashboards are they looking at to prioritize their day? How do they interact with the various fields on the page? What data are they searching for outside Salesforce that you could potentially make more accessible?

If you support Service Cloud, sit with those users to witness the end-to-end case management process. What steps do they take to determine the best way to resolve an issue? Which things seem to take more clicks than they should? What data point would allow them to resolve the matter faster or determine more quickly whether escalation is required?

For each user group you support, ensure you understand what they use Salesforce for and exactly how they use it. Seeing it firsthand is the best way to uncover nitty-gritty challenges and opportunities to smooth out clunky processes.

Watch them work. Notice how they've customized their pages to hide things that aren't relevant. Conversely, if they haven't customized anything and you see that it would be helpful, show them how. Take notes as you observe. You will inevitably have numerous ideas about how quick actions, default field values, dynamic page layouts, and other minor tweaks or feature activations could improve their experiences. These sessions are invaluable in identifying opportunities to reduce clicks or streamline a process, resulting in more selling time or better customer outcomes!

For each of your constituent groups, make sure you've been deskside (virtually or in-person) with at least one user so you can answer these questions:

- Which parts of their job require Salesforce?

- Which features and functionality support their work stream?

- What information do they need from the system?

- Which screens do they access?

- Where are there "swivel chair" steps you can eliminate?

- Which views, reports, or dashboards do they use?

- Which reports do they wish they had?

- What's easy?

- What's difficult?

- What drives them crazy about how the system works?

- What change would provide the most significant impact?

DOS AND DON'TS WHILE DESKSIDE

- **Do** work with applicable team leaders to identify a great candidate to shadow. They will know who can best represent the team and help you steer clear of team members who they expect will express views contrary to management's vision of how they want their team to use the system or raise complaints that don't warrant your attention. This doesn't mean you should only talk to users who are big fans, as it's essential to identify why people aren't using the system and what they don't like about it, but you want to spend time with the *right* detractors.

- **Do** ask open-ended questions to uncover anything you can assist with or that they want to share.

- **Do** solicit ideas. People love to feel like they influenced the solution.

- **Do** get permission if you are going to record your conversation or anything they are doing onscreen.

- **Do** share tips and tricks that would immediately benefit the user.

- **Don't** make promises that you'll make changes. Even if a team member shows you things that are seemingly wonky, promises would be premature. Whether it's a business process or a technical limitation, there may be a valid reason that will preclude you from changing it.

- **Don't** be afraid to say "I don't know, but I'll find out." Then follow up with an answer.

- **Do** keep track of changes you eventually implement based on suggestions from a particular user. Send a note to thank them for their insight. Making sure your users feel listened to and, even better, letting them know you acted on their ideas, goes a long way toward creating your fan club.

Pro tip: Consider other ways to interact with your users, such as regularly hosting a super-user group or having virtual lunch-and-learn sessions. These are excellent ways to develop Salesforce ambassadors representing remote offices and different types of users. These forums provide a bidirectional feedback loop, critical to improving your current system and helping you consider new things to add to the platform.

Spend Time with Functional Leaders

In addition to meeting with users, spend time with functional leaders to understand their priorities and uncover areas of opportunity. This includes the individuals who manage the sales, customer support, and other teams using Salesforce at your company.

You may be apprehensive about scheduling time with these people. After all, they're busy and have big titles, so you might be bothering them, right? Heck no! Done right, their spending time with you is an investment that will yield insightful results. Ideally, these meetings can be an integral part of how you partner with them and help you uncover areas where you can create value, solve problems, and help them achieve their goals.

At a minimum, ask if they will include you in upcoming meetings with their teams so you can see firsthand what information they reference and learn more about their current initiatives. Find out how they use—or, in many cases, don't use—the system to manage their teams. Schedule time with each key manager if your company has multiple team leads, such as regional sales leaders or call center teams that focus on different customer segments. Not only will you expand your network of influence, which can be incredibly helpful when you need feedback or favors, but seeing how leaders use the system will allow you to look holistically at system improvement opportunities.

When meeting with team leaders, start your conversation at the macro level instead of diving into tactical Salesforce topics. What are their big-picture business objectives? What's standing in the way? What performance metrics are they tasked with that you might be able to influence with something in your Salesforce admin arsenal? Do your homework to avoid wasting their time by asking about things you should know. Was a video from the sales kick-off, where sales leaders talked about annual goals, posted on the company intranet? Refer to that and ask follow-up questions. Leading with business issues differentiates you from an order taker.

You can elevate your conversations and business relationships by starting with a broad, open-ended question such as "How's business?" or "What are the pressing issues in your world right now?" While you're at it, don't be afraid to ask outright how you can best add value and other questions to determine how you can support your leaders and their teams.

 # TALK TRACKS:

Sample Questions for Sales Leaders

➢ What strategic initiatives are you focused on this year outside of hitting your numbers?

➢ What sales training or initiatives to reduce ramp time for new hires are in the works?

➢ Which part of your sales cycle has the most room for improvement?

➢ How would you rate pipeline completeness and accuracy?

➢ What would make your reps and sales managers more effective?

TALK TRACKS:

Sample Questions for Customer Support Leaders

➤ What are your service and support priorities?

➤ What are some of your biggest challenges in the customer support process?

➤ What have you identified as gaps between the sales and service hand-off?

➤ What areas in the case resolution process have you identified as a priority?

 TALK TRACKS:

Sample Questions for All Functional Leaders

➤ What is your number one priority right now?

➤ What specific things can I do to add value to your team?

➤ What would you prioritize if you were in my shoes?

➤ What's the most impactful improvement we could make?

➤ Is there anything else I should be asking you?

➤ What's your preferred communication cadence?

Know the Space You Play In

One of the best ways to develop relationships with your functional leaders and position yourself to help them maximize the platform's value is to have familiarity with the business functions you support. This doesn't mean you need to know how to cold call and close a deal to manage Sales Cloud or have call center experience to support Service Cloud, but you should be familiar with the core concepts of sales, marketing, customer support, and other operational processes as applicable.

If Sales Cloud is in your purview, pay attention to trends and hot topics about high-performing sales teams and be fluent in industry practices and strategies related to prospecting, qualifying, and closing deals. Watch what's happening in the RevOps space as the digital customer experience evolves, requiring a more strategic integration of sales, marketing, and customer service.

If Marketing is in the picture, you need to speak the language of demand generation, including understanding key concepts such as lead qualification, click-throughs, and campaign influence. Work for a nonprofit that uses Salesforce for fundraising? Basic concepts related to donor cultivation should be an integral part of your expertise. If you support Service Cloud, you should understand the basic tenets of case management and the types of key performance indicators that drive accomplished customer service teams.

Salesforce admins who came up through the operations side of the business will have an advantage here, but you can quickly develop familiarity and even expertise by reading books, subscribing to blogs, and following a few targeted social media channels. This small investment in time will yield big dividends when you can understand the challenges facing the key leaders you support, and it can propel your relationships with them to new levels.

Know thy Org

As a Salesforce admin, you must know your system from start to finish. The level of effort needed to get a handle on this will depend on how involved you were in designing and building it and the complexity of the system. Either way, make it your mission to familiarize yourself with the application setup. You cannot effectively manage, support, iterate, and improve the platform without an in-depth understanding of what's happening under the hood.

If you are a solo admin, you need to know *it all.* If you work on a large, complex Salesforce implementation and are responsible for only a particular application such as Sales Cloud, or even a subset of functionality within a specific cloud, you may not need to focus on the entire system. Go deep in all areas in your scope of responsibility, including any points of intersection, such as hand-offs between Sales and Service.

If you share Salesforce admin responsibility, you can define areas where each person is the designated SME. Still, I'd encourage you to do enough knowledge sharing and cross-training to ensure that no single person is the only one who knows a part of the system. Making sure someone else knows what you know and can solve critical issues ensures that you can take vacations without calls from the office.

If you were personally involved in setting up the system or if you're managing a system with a relatively straightforward footprint, such as a standard CRM use case, you probably already know your org like the back of your hand. If so, take a quick glance at the list below to confirm that you've got it all down, and then feel free to skip to the next chapter.

If you recently arrived at your job or have an incredibly complex system, it may at first look like the infamous Winchester Mystery House, with rooms full of things that don't make sense and where strange things happen with no reasonable explanation.

Don't panic. You don't need to cram and learn it all in a day. Make sure you've got a handle on the basics and then work your way through the specifics of each object. Review the org to identify areas where you need to focus, then set a goal for when you can reasonably get through it and dedicate time weekly. If you have specific objects or modules in flux, have lots of known issues, or have pending projects, prioritize your deep dive around those areas. From a big-picture perspective, explore which Salesforce components are in use and how the core features have been set up. Leverage the Salesforce Schema Builder to orient yourself to the data model. Then drill deep enough to understand, and ideally, develop documentation for, all the foundational aspects.

Know thy Org Baseline Questions

Users and business use cases

- Which types of licenses are included in your subscription? How many?

- Which objects, tabs, custom apps, and platform features does each team use?

- What profiles are in use, and, at a high level, what are the significant differences between them?

- How is the role hierarchy set up?

What objects are in use in your org? For each object, you should be intimately familiar with the following:

- Security/sharing model

- Record types: Which, why, and how do they differ?

- Record creation: How, when, by whom?

- How are all the fields used and populated? (Consider creating a data dictionary)

- What declarative automation and approval processes exist?

- What validation rules are in place?

- Has the object hit any system limits or is it getting close to hitting any?

- Can you articulate the trigger logic and related actions if code is associated with the object? (Ask a colleague on the Engineering team or a networking contact in the Salesforce Ohana if you need help.)

Integrations

- Which systems are sending or receiving data?

- What's the mechanism?

- What's the frequency?

- What's the business case?

AppExchange apps

- Which packages are installed?

- What is the use case for each and how do they work?

- Are you running the most current version?

 Pro tip: Run the Optimizer App and review the findings to identify defunct architecture, risks to mitigate, places where you are nearing system limitations, and other areas for improvement. While system optimization is never as exciting as rolling out new features, getting your proverbial house in order is a worthwhile investment that will make it easier for you to manage the system over time.

Document thy Org

Consider leveraging the system itself for documentation. One of my standard operating procedures is to add a custom object called Object Overview to memorialize all custom objects, such as what they are, how they work, and why they were created. Given the size limitations when entering the Description field for a custom object and the inability to report on this data, creating a custom object overview record provides much more utility. You can maintain critical documents such as process flows and architectural diagrams as related files or link to them if they reside in a tool such as Confluence. Add fields to capture further details about each object, such as integration, automation, or other things a new Salesforce admin or developer needs to know.

If you have multiple business process owners responsible for signing off on changes on different parts of the system, you can include a junction object to associate the related business user(s) who need to be consulted or informed for each object. Bonus points if you work the Object Overview record into more advanced change-control tracking, such as relating the object overview to another custom object you might use to track system changes and enhancement requests. I'll describe how to do this in Chapter 11.

A Picture for Perspective

Here's an example of using a custom object for system and process documentation in your Salesforce org. Your future self and the admins that come after you will appreciate the time spent capturing this type of information.

Get to Know your Data

As if a deep dive under the hood isn't enough, you must also be familiar with the data. If you don't already have a line of sight into data volumes and the completeness and accuracy of data on your primary objects, build dashboards to see at-a-glance metrics such as the number of records by record type for a given object.

A small number of records on particular objects may indicate an adoption issue or identify a defunct system infrastructure. Objects with extremely high data volumes may indicate a need for system optimization, such as custom indexing, to ensure no performance issues. Use free tools from the AppExchange to report on field usage. Having insight into the data quality will inevitably yield ideas about improving the system that you can bring to your stakeholders for discussion.

When reporting on data, watch out for a few known gotchas that have stymied many a Salesforce admin:

- Your results will not include closed activities more than a year old, as those are automatically archived to improve the speed and performance of Activity reports. (Hint: you can log a case with Salesforce to increase the time before activities are archived.)

- When reporting on the Contact object, the standard contact reports exclude any that do not have an associated Account record. These are considered private records, which means they're only included if the Contact Owner is the running user. Again, you can use the Data Loader to export these or create a list view on the Contact tab to see if you have any. Interestingly, these private contacts will appear when you run a list view if you add a filter to show records where the Account Name field is blank.

Pro tip: Get to know your Salesforce subscription, including reading your contract to understand precisely which functionality each license type includes. Over the years, Salesforce has made significant changes. If your org has been around for a while, you may have grandfathered-in functionality that would otherwise have an associated cost. Conversely, you may assume certain features are available that may not be due to the license type or contractual restrictions.

Table Stakes Wrap-Up

We've reviewed the prerequisites to setting yourself up for success as an exceptional Salesforce admin. For the record, these are not activities you do once and never have to do again. Try incorporating these activities into your standard operating procedures to stay on top of new initiatives, shifting priorities, and changes within your company and your Salesforce org.

- Spend time learning about your company's mission, significant initiatives, key metrics, and any relevant industry nuances.

- Spend time with your stakeholders to learn their objectives, business processes, and key performance indicators.

- Interact with your users to understand how they work, what's important to them, and how they are (or are not) using the system.

- Develop some expertise around key sales concepts if you support the sales team—ditto for any other processes you support.

- Dig in to understand how the system was designed and configured.

These steps will position you to provide relevant and targeted advice to your stakeholders. Keep reading to discover how great Salesforce admins leverage their knowledge to deliver significant value and create a cadre of raving fans.

CHAPTER 3:

PROBE TO FIND OUT WHAT THEY REALLY NEED

A prudent question is one-half of wisdom.

—Francis Bacon

Now let's dive into the specific behaviors and competencies that will establish your domain expertise and make you an indispensable Salesforce admin pro. Depending on how you arrived at your current gig, you may already excel at these skills or find that they come naturally to you. For instance, if you've spent time embedded with sales teams—a common path for many Sales Cloud admins—you may already be good at asking probing questions to uncover business challenges. If you were a Salesforce user before deciding to make a career of it, you know a lot about the features that gave you value, which ones were vexing, and which would benefit your current constituents. In this case, you will likely find it easier to identify problems to solve and communicate how the teams you support can extract more value from the platform.

Maybe you arrived in the Salesforce admin role as the first step on a new career path. (Big shout-out to you veterans, seniors, returning workers, and others who chose to learn Salesforce from a completely different line of work.) For you, some of these activities may be less intuitive. But the good news is that these aren't vague ideas; they're specific skills and behaviors you can learn, practice, and perfect. And these skills and behaviors build on each other, so as you ace one, you can better address the others on your list, creating a snowball effect of value.

As we explore other critical competencies in subsequent chapters, you'll see that nailing this first competency, probing to uncover the real business need, is essential in all the Salesforce admin pro competencies.

First, Put On Your Business Analyst Hat

One of the many hats Salesforce admins wear is that of the business analyst (BA). According to the International Institute of Business Analysis, this function is "the practice of enabling change in an organizational context, by defining needs and recommending solutions that deliver value to stakeholders."[3]

Sound similar to the work you do? The BA role is distinct from the Salesforce admin role in many organizations, where BAs may be assigned to work with business stakeholders on larger projects.

Trailhead includes an entire module for the Salesforce business analyst, a role described there as helping "guide the business to improve business processes and efficiency in Salesforce. They elicit, document, and analyze requirements around business challenges, and then produce data-driven solutions."[4] Do any of these activities resonate with you?

Whether or not there are dedicated BAs on your team, effectively incorporating business analysis as an inherent part of your job is one way to differentiate yourself as a stand-out Salesforce admin. The best way to prove you aren't just an order taker is by demonstrating that you don't just take orders. Whether working on a simple change request or participating in a significant system enhancement, you probe to ensure that you understand the ask. You dig deep for the business context and desired outcome. And only then do you carefully consider the best solution.

Cue the Rolling Stones, as you may need to summon your inner Mick Jagger to get comfortable with the idea that your constituents can't always get what they want. Your job is to determine the problem they're trying to solve to ensure they get what they need.

This chapter provides techniques for honing the essential BA skills of eliciting requirements and understanding the critical context to ensure that you deliver the right solution. First we'll look at a few examples to illustrate why what constituents ask for and what they end up with often look decidedly different. Then we'll cover approaches and what to say to help you uncover the true need.

Why a Request for a Checkbox Seldom Results in Adding a Checkbox

I can't tell you how often I've heard something along the lines of "We just need to add a checkbox." If I had a dollar for every time I assessed the request and ultimately added this field, I might be able to treat one friend to coffee. On the other hand, if I had a dollar for all the times the solution ended up being something entirely different and often more complicated, I could treat several friends to a fancy dinner!

Why is that the case? Often, the new field they want to add probably shouldn't be a checkbox. Depending on the use case, it's likely that another field type, such as a picklist, would be a better way to capture the data. The other reason is that when you dig in to understand the impetus for the request and what they are trying to accomplish, you'll often find that the solution requires something entirely different than adding a field. In hindsight, I wish I'd saved all those "I just need a field" requests over the years to laugh about some very complex solutions delivered once we dug into the why.

Now let's walk through two hypothetical scenarios so you can see how to uncover what's really needed when you receive this type of request.

Scenario 1: A different field type would be a better solution.

"Please add a checkbox called 'Has Pets?' to the contact record."

Let's say you work for a foundation and received this request from Miguel, the development director. He's the Salesforce application owner for your organization, so this is an authorized request, but is it the right approach?

Probably not. If you are a relatively new Salesforce admin, you may not yet have an aversion to checkboxes for this type of use case, so here's the deal: users love them because they're easy to check and look good on the page, but two issues inevitably arise. First, there's no way to make the field required without requiring the box to be checked. As a result, you don't know if the user intended to leave the field blank or neglected to check the box. Second, because checkboxes return as "0" or "1" in reports, this can cause heartburn for users and result in requests for formula fields to translate the data into something more user-friendly for reporting. That means more work for you and more redundant fields to maintain.

You walk down the hall for a quick chat with Miguel to uncover the impetus behind the ask.

"I'm following up on your request," you say. "It looks pretty straightforward, but I'd love to understand the context. How will you use this new data point?"

Miguel explains that he wants to capture additional details about the donors in order to be more targeted in future fundraising efforts. He wants to run different campaigns depending on whether or not people have pets.

You ask, "Who will be responsible for entering the data?"

He says the three fundraising coordinators on his team will make calls in their respective regions. He explains that he plans to run a contest; they'll call as many donors as possible in the next two weeks to capture this information.

"One more question," you say. "I'm curious if you've thought about how you'll be able to differentiate between donors missing a response to that question versus donors who indicated that they don't have pets?" While you're talking, you do a quick sketch on the whiteboard.

The lightbulb goes on over Miguel's head as he realizes the solution he asked for wouldn't quite meet his needs.

Instead of a checkbox, you recommend a yes/no picklist and explain why this type of field will work better. Miguel agrees. By ensuring that you understood the request and what was driving it, you've solved a problem he didn't even know he was about to have. We'll discuss this way of adding value in a future chapter.

A Picture for Perspective

There is no way to tell if this field is blank because the donor has no pets or because this data point has not been validated. Additionally, unless the desired behavior is that users always check the box, there is no way to require a value.

A picklist provides a way to differentiate blank records from those a user has populated with a value of "No" and allows options for making a field required to ensure that the data is collected.

Scenario 2: The right solution is more complex than just adding a field.

"Please add a checkbox called 'Proposal Sent' on the Opportunity record below the Stage field. It should be editable by all sales reps."

Suppose this request comes into your queue somewhat out of the blue, as you haven't been privy to any conversations regarding changes to the proposal process. Before you do anything, you'll need to determine if this person is authorized to make the request. Just because a sales rep or other user wants to add a new field or make a change doesn't mean you should. You confirm that the request came from Ritika, who is authorized to request changes as a senior sales leader. From a configuration standpoint, this falls into the quick-hit category, and, besides, can't you assume that a senior sales leader knows exactly what's needed? Maybe, but let's play this out.

You reach out to Ritika, ideally in person if you're at the same office location, or by phone if you're remote, as a live conversation is much needed when eliciting business requirements.

"Hi Ritika, I'm following up on your request. It looks pretty straightforward, but I'd love to get some context. Can you share what prompted this ask?"

She explains that she's seen a high number of lost sales lately. She is trying to understand whether they are losing deals before they even have a chance to deliver the final proposal or if they are primarily getting cut in the final round.

"That makes sense. I'm curious, what's your hypothesis?"

She thinks her team isn't making it to the shortlist enough. They engage with many prospects but seem to be getting cut before the final bid process. She says her colleague, who manages the Western region, thinks it's more likely their proposals are of poor quality; he blames that for their low win rate.

You ask, "How are you planning to use this new data point?"

"It will help us determine where we are losing deals in the sales cycle," she answers. "Depending on what we learn, we'll need to provide our teams with more training in the front half of the selling process, or we may need to work with our proposal team. Maybe both. In any event, it's important, so we want to get it right."

"Have you looked at any stage history reports?"

She responds, "What are those?"

You move forward with questions but note that you need to explore this feature with her as soon as possible.

"By the way," you add, "How do you envision this field getting populated?"

Ritika walks through the current process, describing how the proposal team emails the sales rep when the proposal is complete and uploads it to Files. The rep then attaches it to an email and sends it to the prospect. She explains that they will instruct the reps to manually check the box to confirm that they have sent it.

Hmmm. Reps have to check the box? You know from experience it's unlikely they'll remember to do this. This process is screaming for some automation.

I'm willing to bet that by now, you have gears grinding and plenty of questions you want to ask. What are the existing opportunity stages? Shouldn't that field already be able to provide this information? Why isn't there more automation in the proposal process? You're probably thinking through all the things in your Salesforce admin bag of tricks that you could apply. While you don't yet have enough information in this hypothetical scenario to prescribe the right approach, it's evident that there are various ways to attack Ritika's stated problem and the underlying process issues.

Adding a checkbox is likely not the best path forward. Instead, you arrange to meet with Ritika the following day. You can walk her through a few reports to provide some immediate insight and dive deeper into the proposal process to determine a more robust solution.

Voila! By engaging in business conversation instead of immediately responding to the ask, you've demonstrated that you're a value-adding consultant, not an order taker.

These two scenarios illustrate why even the most straightforward change requests warrant due diligence. A solid understanding of the business drivers becomes even more critical when you're tasked with more extensive enhancements or standing up net-new functionality. Your stakeholders have expertise in sales, customer service, or whatever function their job entails. They're not experts on the Salesforce platform and can't possibly know all the options, implications, or considerations involved in determining the best solution. They don't know if adding a checkbox is the right course of action. Nor should they. Their job is to provide the business context to allow you to understand what they want to accomplish and why. The onus is on you to separate the real issue and desired outcome from their stated request and then determine how to proceed. Sometimes this means you must tactfully challenge assumptions and ask hard questions, or at least summon your inner three-year-old to keep asking questions until you learn the why.

Of course, we can't hammer our peeps with a literal barrage of "Why? Why? Why?" While a three-year-old can discern plenty of information this way, it's annoying, off-putting, and likely to end in an exasperated "Because I said so!"

Instead, here are compelling open-ended questions you can ask in a consultative and professional manner. Leading with a few of these will help you uncover what's behind the ask and help keep your stakeholder focused on outcomes instead of functionality.

 ## TALK TRACKS:

15 Questions to Elicit Requirements

➢ Help me understand what you're trying to accomplish.

➢ What's your end game?

➢ What's driving this request?

➢ Please provide more background for context.

➢ Walk me through the issues you're trying to address.

➢ How do you do this today?

➢ How does this fit into your current process?

➢ What part of this would you describe as a must-have versus a nice-to-have?

➢ How are you tracking this today?

➢ What will success look like? How will you measure that?

➢ Who else might be impacted by this change?

➢ Where does this fall on your priority list?

➢ What's driving that priority?

➢ What concerns do you have?

➢ What have we not discussed that you think is important?

➢ Why now?

In addition to using these open-ended questions as conversation starters, you'll be amazed by what else you can elicit with a few more strategic open-ended questions peppered throughout your conversation. You want your brain cells actively listening, not focused on what you'll say next, so practice having a few easy questions on the tip of your tongue. I'm partial to "What else?" or "Tell me more." These are a few oldies but goodies I've kept from my days as a sales trainer, as the discovery skills required for sales professionals mirror the questioning skills required for Salesforce admins. (Hint: If you work with salespeople and have the opportunity to sit in on their training sessions, do it.)

As you listen, ask for clarification if there is complexity or something you aren't following. Say, "Time out. I want to make sure I understand" or "Can you provide some concrete examples?" Don't worry that you will look bad. Your colleagues will appreciate your efforts to get to know their business process. Be genuinely curious and make sure you understand the answers to any relevant questions. Once you have a solid understanding of the issues, repeat what you heard for confirmation.

 ## TALK TRACKS:

Confirming Your Understanding

➤ Let me play that back…

➤ I'd like to confirm my understanding…

➤ To ensure that we're on the same page…

➤ Let me say that back to you to make sure I've got it…

 Pro tip: Probing to understand the use case is not limited to requests for new features or functionality. Anything new that comes into your queue, including report requests, warrants the same curiosity about the impetus and desired output. For example, a report built on the Accounts with Cases report type will yield different results than Accounts with or without Cases. Your questions will ensure that the report parameters return the expected results. Plus, you may uncover that the report is related to a particular challenge or a new focus area, allowing you an opportunity to introduce other Salesforce solutions and work your admin magic.

A Real-Life Example

Questions you get asked about the system also warrant curiosity. The simple phrase, "I'm curious, why do you ask?" can yield valuable insight. I recall a support ticket submitted asking "What time does the integration with our financial system run?" An admin on the team responded that the integration runs in real-time when a record is saved, then quickly closed the ticket. When I saw the subject line on this closed case, it caught my attention. *Why was someone asking this?* I asked the team member to follow up and see what had prompted the question, as it likely indicated either a problem with the integration or a process or training gap.

Sure enough, they were attempting to figure out why specific currency fields on their Account record were out of sync. After some investigation, we confirmed that the integration had stalled. We would have been alerted eventually, but we missed a critical opportunity to solve a problem for a user and proactively identify a technical issue by not asking the question.

We've now covered the importance of truly understanding the business problem, desired outcome, and the reason behind the ask before putting hands on keyboards. In some cases, your questions will confirm that the functionality requested is the right solution so that you can confidently execute it. In other cases, your findings may lead you to a different conclusion. Eventually, as your stakeholders understand your approach and realize its value, you'll hear less about checkboxes and more "I need your help with a business problem. Can we talk?"

CHAPTER 4:

PROVIDE EXPERT ADVICE

Incompetence is certainty in the absence of expertise.
Overconfidence is certainty in the presence of expertise.

—Malcolm Gladwell

The *Merriam-Webster* dictionary defines expertise as an expert's skill and the expression of an expert opinion or commentary. Fittingly, your expertise will be measured both by your Salesforce platform know-how and your ability to translate that into guidance and direction for your business partners. Your ability to uncover business outcomes coupled with your Salesforce platform skills will position you as an authority, regardless of your title. Your stakeholders will perceive you as a trusted advisor rather than an order taker when you help them understand and assess options. You will garner domain authority by demonstrating how to best leverage the platform's capabilities to accomplish their business objectives.

Beware of Being Too Literal

Thanks to the Salesforce platform's flexibility, the best solution for a particular use case is not always cut and dried. There are usually multiple ways to solve a problem, each with many pros and cons. Even the Salesforce standard objects, available out of the box to support specific business processes, may or may not make sense in relation to particular business requirements. You may be tempted to jump in and start solutioning, especially when a request refers to specific functionality, as you want to be responsive. Still, it's essential to understand the *what* and *why* before assuming the *how*. Armed with that information, you can apply your Salesforce knowledge and thoughtfully consider all the options that the platform presents.

Let's look at a few examples of common business requests:

- "We need tasks to track our work."

- "We would like better visibility into our leads."

- "We need a place to put notes."

These are examples in which the ask sounds like a Salesforce feature. An order taker might hear these requests, bust out Activities, expose the Leads tab, and add the Notes object to every page. Is that wrong? Not necessarily, but just because the words match some out-of-the-box thing in Salesforce doesn't necessarily make it the right solution. After researching the desired business outcome, you may find that the solution doesn't warrant that specific functionality.

In some cases, the person who made the request won't know that there is Salesforce functionality called Notes or Leads or whatever else they're requesting. They will merely state their business problem with no expectation about what the solution looks like, and they won't care as long as it meets their needs. In other cases, your business partner may have learned about certain functionality from a webinar or sales presentation by their Salesforce account team, and they'll have a preconceived idea about how that specific thing will solve their problem. Or maybe they used the feature when they worked in a different company. Regardless of the situation, if you've probed to confirm the need and know the thing asked for is not the right solution, you can establish your expertise by explaining your rationale and demonstrating a better path forward. You may feel uncomfortable proposing alternatives, but as your approach proves out with a few wins on the board, your stakeholders will begin to trust that you'll figure out the *how* if they explain the what and why.

Is Salesforce Notes the Right Solution?

"We need a place to put notes."

Let's say you get this request from one of your business teams. Does this mean you should implement the out-of-the-box Salesforce Notes feature?

The Notes functionality can be an excellent tool for keeping users organized. It can allow the addition of rich text, images, and all sorts of content. Users can even see and revert to prior versions if they're working in Lightning.

That's good stuff, but when you drill into precisely what problem they're trying to solve, you may find that they're looking for a more confined, structured field on the detail page of a record. They may need to see those notes included in reports and list views for that object. So the first order of business is to put on your BA hat and do a little digging, or discovery, as it's often called.

 TALK TRACKS:

Sample Discovery Questions

➢ Tell me more about the notes you need to capture. What type of content would your team include? Can you provide examples?

➢ Who would be entering these notes, and under what circumstances?

➢ Is this a new process? If not, how is it being done today?

➢ Is a note required at a certain point in the process? If so, when?

➢ Will the content of the notes change over time? Do we need to retain a history of the prior version?

> ➤ What are the requirements for understanding who entered the note? Do we need to track when it was entered or last modified?

> ➤ Would plain text suffice, or is there a need to capture rich text or images?

> ➤ Talk to me about the size of the notes field. Do you have a sense of how many characters are needed?

> ➤ Where does that information need to be visible in the system?

> ➤ What are the reporting requirements?

Can you see how you might arrive at an entirely different conclusion depending on the answers?

Perhaps they describe a scenario for which they need to capture a few sentences to add color to the Status field, maybe even requiring that users enter an explanation for a given status value. In this case, a text area field coupled with a validation rule is probably the right approach.

Perhaps they explain that the people on the team involved in this business process need to record various ad-hoc comments and ideas they receive and simply want a consistent place to find the information should they need to refer to it after the fact. In that case, the Notes functionality is probably the right fit.

Or suppose they explain that the notes they want to track are the meeting minutes taken at events already being captured as Activity records. In that case, maybe you suggest uploading a file or pasting the text into a field in the event record.

There's no one-size-fits-all answer. Your expertise in understanding the ask and applying your platform knowledge will ensure they get what they need.

Would using Leads Meet the Needs?

"We need better visibility into our leads."

Suppose this request comes from your sales leader. Should you turn on the Sales Cloud Lead Management feature? Again, it depends. There's nothing inherently wrong with this approach. I've helped dozens of companies implement the Leads functionality. The Lead object offers tremendous benefits as a holding tank to qualify and dedupe company and contact records before including them in the central database. The Leads functionality includes sophisticated features, such as web-to-lead automation, lead queues, assignment rules, and integration with Salesforce Campaigns.

However, depending on what your business partner means by "better visibility into leads," introducing the Lead object may be more trouble than it's worth or may not scratch the right itch. The Leads functionality generally has less utility when the same team does both demand generation and sales. In that case, it's often not intuitive to sales reps that their leads exist in separate reports and views from their opportunities. Furthermore, activating this feature requires significant training on the entire dedupe and conversion process.

You do some thoughtful probing to follow up on this request. You uncover that the reps are using spreadsheets to track their early-stage deals, specifically "suspects" they've started calling on, but they've gotten little or no traction. Sales management has been adamant that the pipeline should only include qualified deals, so the reps are reluctant to enter these early deals because they don't yet meet the stated definition required for the first sales stage, which has a 10 percent probability. You confirm that sales managers want to keep these "almost deals" off of dashboards to ensure that their sales pipelines are not full of pipe dreams, but they do want to understand where their reps are prospecting.

You consider the options, including reviewing the benefits of having the reps enter Lead records and then convert them at the appropriate time in the sales cycle. After much analysis, you determine that the business process doesn't warrant all the bells and whistles included with the Leads functionality, so the benefit of using Leads won't justify rolling them out. Instead, you propose adding a new Opportunity stage specifically for unqualified deals. This value will map to a 0 percent probability, which means they will be omitted from the forecast. These deals can be filtered out of management reports and dashboards but will provide a seamless experience for reps who can track all their pursuits, regardless of the stage, in one place. With this approach, sales managers will have new dashboard widgets to report on these 0 percent deals, allowing them to see the top of the funnel without mucking up the actual pipeline.

You present the recommendation to the sales leaders, including a brief discussion of the options you considered. You also share some implications you will have to address, such as the fact that this change will impact metrics, as the Opportunity Age will now include the qualification period. You recommend adding a new field to calculate the age of the deals starting when they reach the qualification stage. They agree that your overall approach seems reasonable without much heavy lifting or excessive training required.

Abracadabra! You've not only saved yourself a ton of work by recommending the path of least resistance, but you've also demonstrated your ability to identify the best "right-sized" solution to the problem.

Questions around how and when Sales Cloud customers should use the standard Leads functionality can be a hot topic in the Salesforce community as there isn't a one-size-fits-all approach. In some cases, it makes sense that certain sales or demand gen teams will log activities at the lead level. In other cases, it makes sense to use the lead object only as a holding tank to get prospects loaded into the database before they are de-duped and confirmed to belong to a valid target company. In some instances, the lead object might not be warranted at all. This scenario wasn't intended to dive into all the considerations as much to drive home the fact that just because someone says they need to "see leads," they don't *necessarily* need to activate the Leads functionality.

A Real-Life Example

I recall a Salesforce admin who once went deep into the weeds after a sales leader emailed requesting assistance "setting up territories." After many wasted hours trying to get up to speed on Enterprise Territory Management, he finally picked up the phone and talked with the sales leader to determine what problem she was trying to solve. She was simply looking for a more robust way to differentiate the regional sales teams within the existing role hierarchy. For that, activating Territory Management definitely would have been overkill.

I've had similar conversations related to the topic of sales forecasting. The forecasting process looks entirely different from company to company. When tasked with implementing or improving a forecast process to get to the critical questions of how much to expect and when to expect it, the circumstances may or may not warrant implementing the Collaborative Forecast feature. Savvy Salesforce admins must be discerning when evaluating each unique situation. Determining the best approach by applying platform expertise and avoiding solutions more complex than needed are critical elements to creating value.

Communicating your Recommendations

What happens when your stakeholders push hard for a particular feature but you aren't sure it's the correct answer?

Let's consider the request for better lead visibility. Suppose the sales leader who asked for that previously used the Lead object, so that's all she knows. She may be resistant to doing something different or be unable to visualize an alternative solution. It's perfectly acceptable to say "I'll do some digging and get back to you on that." Then do the research. Have an open mind regarding the pros and cons of different options.

Someone once told me there are six ways to do things in Salesforce, but you won't know which one is right or wrong until a year later. Phone a friend or post your scenario online and let other Trailblazers keep you honest. Whether the request is related to big new pieces of functionality or small incremental tweaks, what's important is understanding what they are trying to accomplish, thoroughly reviewing the options, and then confidently communicating your findings to your stakeholders.

Your business partners will value your ability to explain options in easily understood terms, including each option's ramifications or benefits. Present the possible approaches or recommended solutions in an organized, concise way to communicate the implications of choosing one path over another. Confirm what was requested, including what you learned about the stated problem or desired business outcome. Sometimes you will be agnostic and present several options, with pros and cons for your stakeholders to consider. Other times, you'll have a definite point of view, in which case you'll need to clearly state your recommendation, including the business and technical considerations that led to your conclusion. If you have a proposed approach, lead with that and include the alternatives considered and rationale for your recommendation. Most importantly, make sure it's clear you listened to the original request and the reason behind it to craft the best solution.

 Pro tip: Besides sharing the information with your stakeholders, take time to document the technical pros and cons of alternative approaches, noting any considerations you made that impacted your approach. Did you make a particular design decision because you hit a system limit? Was there a specific requirement that sealed the deal based on how the functionality worked? Your future self will not remember the details when the question arises again, and future admins who arrive after you leave will appreciate the context!

Now let's consider one more hypothetical scenario to illustrate how to combine your business analysis skills and platform expertise to arrive at the best solution.

Franchise Management Scenario, Part 1

"We need to add a few fields to the Account record."

Let's say you work for a retail company that franchises its operations. Gwen, the communications manager who works with the franchisees, calls to discuss some new fields she would like you to add to the Account record. She explains that they are launching a new certification program to ensure franchisees remain updated on company policies and marketing promotions. Gwen is a hands-on Salesforce user, so she's specific: "We need a date field called Most Recent Certification Date, a picklist called Certification Type, a picklist called Certification Status, and a percent field to capture their certification score."

Phew! At least she didn't ask for a checkbox. She shared the rationale for the request: she's launching a new program. Because she's provided context and clarity about what she needs, can't you just start knocking this out for her?

Maybe, but let's see what else you can uncover with a few probing questions.

"So, Gwen, I'm curious about the concept of the *most recent* certification date. How often do you expect that they will get certified?"

She explains that the specifics of how the program will work on an ongoing basis are in flux, but it is likely to be an annual process. They are also considering certification programs specific to various topics, such as safety, marketing, and compliance.

You ask, "Is it fair to assume you'd want to maintain the details about their prior certifications?"

"Yes," she says, "we might even incorporate all their certifications in our annual award ceremony at the franchisee summit. Eventually, we'll have awards for the highest score, the most certifications obtained, and things like that."

Ding ding ding! You've crossed into that territory where the solution may look different than the ask. Because she described a one-to-many relationship between the franchisees and the certifications they will obtain, you quickly assess that creating a new custom object makes sense rather than capturing the data in fields on the Account record as per her request. You can see the data model in your mind and quickly start sketching it out.

You confirm your understanding of the requirements and tell her you have a good sense of how you can support this. "Gwen, I have an idea of how to do this in a manner that will be slightly different than what you asked for but will meet your needs and be a much more scalable solution. Is it okay if I take some creative license to address this?"

Setting the stage that you're going off-script lets you know how attached your stakeholder is to a predetermined solution. Resistance here would warrant more questions and certainly more conversation if your proposed solution ends up not being an exact match with the request.

In this case, Gwen indicates that she trusts your judgment and says she's excited to see what you come up with. You believe this will be a quick configuration exercise, so you'd rather demonstrate the proposed solution than explain it in detail now. If this were a complicated build or a request that required significant time-consuming automation, it would be vital that you agree on the approach in more detail before putting hands on keyboard for anything other than a quick mockup.

A Picture for Perspective

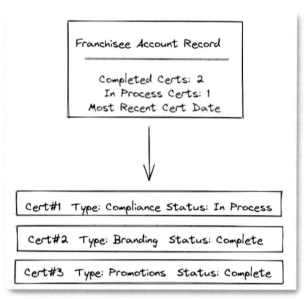

Since there will be a one-to-many relationship between franchisees and their certifications, adding a new custom object with a relationship to the Account is a more scalable approach than capturing certification details directly in the Account record.

You can aggregate information on the Account to provide high-level metrics across all the certification records, including salient data points such as the most recent certification date or counts of relevant records.

Franchise Management Scenario, Part 2

As you wrap up your call with Gwen, let's suppose you ask one more open-ended question: "What else do I need to know to support this initiative?" She replies, "Thank you. I almost forgot to mention that we will need to set up tasks so the certification specialist knows which accounts they are assigned to certify, and so we can track their progress."

Like requests related to notes and leads, a request for tasks may or may not warrant using the standard Task record that's part of the Salesforce out-of-the-box Activity functionality. Using the standard Activity objects makes perfect sense for tracking actions such as phone calls and meetings, but certain types of assignments may warrant an alternative solution, such as using the Owner field in the record to indicate this or adding a custom user lookup field combined with a picklist to track a status value. So, once again, you don your BA hat and dig into the details.

 ## TALK TRACKS:

Sample Discovery Questions

➤ How will the certification specialists be assigned?

➤ Can you walk me through how the team will use tasks?

➤ How will the certification specialists communicate with their accounts?

➤ What are your expectations for the certification specialists regarding tracking phone calls and emails?

➤ Are there requirements or expectations regarding specific activity levels?

➤ Do the certification specialists currently use the standard Activity records to support other parts of their role?

➤ How will you measure their success—do they have KPIs or activity metrics?

As you continue your discussion with Gwen, you learn that the certification specialists currently use the Activity timeline to track conversations and emails. However, that is entirely at their discretion, and they do not have specific activity metrics. With this understanding, you determine that it makes sense to include the timeline on the Certification page layout so the team can track their calls and correspondence, but you conclude that the task record isn't the best mechanism for monitoring certification responsibility or the status of the certification process. Instead, you've added to the Certification object a lookup field pointing to the User record to track the person assigned and a status field to track progress.

A Picture for Perspective

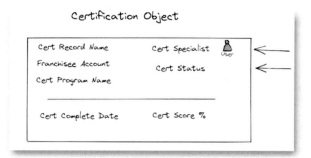

Adding fields for the assigned certification specialist and status directly to the Certification object will provide easier reporting than capturing that information on Task records, which can still be used to manage calls, emails, and meetings relating to the process.

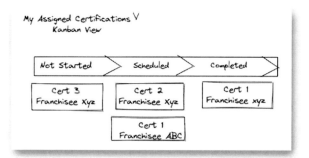

Certification specialists can use reports and list views on the Certification tab to track their assignments, as seen in this Kanban view.

A few days later, you meet with Gwen. You review her request and confirm your understanding of the what and why. You walk her through a demo of the new custom object, which you've loaded with sample data to paint a vivid picture. Next, you tell her why you determined that a new custom object was the right solution, pointing out the one-to-many relationship between the records and demonstrating multiple types of certifications tracked for the sample company record you are using. You pause to give her a few minutes to absorb what you're showing her.

You highlight a few "bonus features" you've included, such as roll-up summary fields in the company record to count the number of certifications, a Path, and a graphic to indicate a completed certification. (Bonus features are items that weren't specifically requested that improve the solution or enhance usability. I cover them in detail in Chapter 9.) Lastly, you point out that the Activity timeline is on the page layout to track interactions with the franchisees. You share that you believe there's a better approach for tracking certification assignments and completion. You show Gwen a Kanban-style list view to demonstrate how her team can track their work, initiating the virtual confetti when you use the Path to mark the status complete.

You encourage Gwen to ask questions, pause to let her take it all in, and then ask if the solution meets her needs.

"Absolutely! Even better than I expected. I didn't realize that there was so much I'd want to track as part of this program," she says. "And now that I see it in action, I have some additional ideas I'd like to explore with you."

Ka-ching! Your value-creation points are on the rise. Once again, your ability to understand the business objectives and then provide expert advice to help accomplish them demonstrates that you are a business partner, not an order taker.

DOS AND DON'TS:
SOLUTIONING WITH THE END IN MIND

- **Do** ask questions to understand the big picture, the context of the requirements, and the expected business outcomes.

- **Do** confirm your understanding of what your business partners want to accomplish.

- **Do** communicate and make sure they understand the reason—most importantly, how they'll benefit—if your proposed solution looks different from the ask.

- **Do** make sure you have buy-in and agreement before proceeding. You don't want to find out after the fact that your stakeholders felt like they weren't listened to or you didn't meet their needs.

- **Don't** believe you have to solve any problem on the spot. It's okay to say something along the lines of "Now that I have a good idea of what you're trying to accomplish, I'll get back to you shortly with my recommended approach."

CHAPTER 5:

PRODUCE DATA INSIGHTS AND ACTIONABLE IDEAS

It is a capital mistake to theorize before one has data.

—Sherlock Holmes

Chapter 4 covered how to apply your questioning skills and platform expertise to ensure that your design decisions and proposed solutions will effectively meet the business's needs. You can also deliver a ton of value by ensuring that your constituents have the awareness and understanding to fully leverage the tools they already have at their fingertips, including available features and functionality and all the valuable insights the data can provide. Extra credit if you can help them uncover critical insight from the data and pair that with a specific Salesforce solution to deliver tangible business outcomes. Helping your stakeholders wring more value from the Salesforce platform is another powerful way to make your mark.

There's Data Gold in Them Thar Hills!

Salesforce's analytics capabilities have come a long way due to significant enhancements to Einstein Analytics, rebranded as CRM Analytics, and the acquisition of Tableau. If you have the good fortune to work for a company that leverages one or both of these tools, you have an excellent opportunity to blow minds as you help your constituents visualize and understand data. Time spent learning these is a worthwhile investment that will increase your value.

Fear not if you don't have access to either of them. You still have ample opportunities to help your constituents leverage Salesforce data to gain insight and understanding. Even as Salesforce's analytics capabilities have dramatically improved, I'm willing to bet that many of your users, including your functional leaders, are barely scratching the surface regarding what they can glean from even the most basic Salesforce reports and dashboards.

Whether you specialize in Sales Cloud, Service Cloud, or any other part of the platform, you're sitting on a veritable data gold mine. There is information in the system that can make your business run better. Somewhere in there are nuggets of actionable insight that will help you shed light on all kinds of issues and help your organization make critical business decisions.

What's working? What's not? Which customers need more attention? Which products are outperforming, and which ones are duds? Which donors need more cultivating? Which reps need more coaching, and on what topics?

Illuminating this information contributes to your reputation as a collaborative, knowledgeable business partner. Putting your BA skills to work means not only generating requested reports but identifying where there may be information gaps and helping them answer the "So What?" question each report reveals.

Take a moment to consider your system. Are there key reports no one is using? What components could you add to a dashboard to illustrate a trend or illuminate a problem? What new metrics could add color or highlight something that warrants attention? Conversely, where could you leverage Salesforce tools such as conditional formatting to color-code an existing report or dashboard widget to make it easier to understand the data?

Not only will you have business stakeholders who do not understand how to leverage the data for actionable insight, you'll likely have some who struggle to get their hands on it. A little training in this regard can go a long way.

Although Salesforce enables users to build their own reports, it's a good idea to cultivate and maintain a core set of reports for each department's primary reporting needs. Because there are significant differences between report results depending on the report type used, try to eliminate the need for anyone other than Super Users or those with in-depth report training to build a report from scratch. Instead, set up reports for the various types of data they will most likely need, adding relevant fields and putting them in a logical order. Then, invest the time to train them on basic reporting skills, including how to slice and dice such that one single report can give them all sorts of insights. Giving all users, especially your team leaders, the know-how to drill down, change dates, summarize by different fields, and make other report tweaks is a win-win. They get value and you get fewer requests as they learn to self serve.

I've spent the bulk of my career working with sales organizations, so the first few examples are a bit Sales Cloud–centric, but the principles apply across the board. Some constituents may need help comprehending data even if you present it on a knocked-out dashboard. Functional team leaders often don't realize the breadth of information at their fingertips or know how to tie it to their business objectives. You can make a significant impact by demonstrating the types of available reports and insights each can provide. Your value-add multiplies when you not only help them dig into the data but follow up with recommendations for how they can leverage the Salesforce platform to act on it.

So They've Got a Dashboard. Now What?

Everyone knows sales leaders should use Salesforce dashboards to manage their pipelines and lead team meetings, right? Nonetheless, I can't tell you how many hours I've spent showing sales leaders how to use them to manage and coach their teams. Running a sales meeting using a dashboard instead of a spreadsheet is not necessarily intuitive. Your team leads may not know what they should be paying attention to in the system.

I see this with sales leaders at all levels, especially with newly-promoted front-line sales managers, who may have used Salesforce as a rep but don't have a clue how to leverage it as a management tool. In my experience, most companies skimp on providing managers with the training to fully utilize Salesforce for coaching, so managers often don't have a clear idea of what to look at besides reviewing pipeline reports. If there's not a standard suite of dashboards for all managers, work with them to create one. If a functional leader is experiencing specific challenges, create a dashboard or set of reports that surface actionable information. You'll earn significant Salesforce superhero cred if you help them see how Salesforce data can help them identify corrective action and coaching areas to improve their team's performance.

Don't just show what reports to run. Help explain the "So what?" based on what the data is saying.

Sample Scenario 1

"We need to sign more net-new clients."

Let's say you are meeting with Laura, one of your sales managers. You're doing a great job asking open-ended questions about her business, and you uncover that she's getting pressured to bring in more net-new clients. She says her sales reps are successfully growing their footprints with existing customers but have signed relatively few new logos this year.

"Why do you think that is?"

She replies candidly, "I really don't know." She shares a few questions she's been thinking about that might illuminate what's behind the low numbers. "I wonder if the team is so busy taking care of our existing clients that they aren't spending enough time prospecting into new accounts. Or perhaps we are leading with the wrong service when selling to a new prospect."

You take notes, confirm your understanding, and then walk her through a few reports to provide insight, explicitly pointing out the link between the questions she's raised and each report's answers. You offer to put a dashboard together so she can easily access and track the key data points. You get big points for the recommendation that it include a leaderboard to ensure that the team applies collective focus to the pursuit of new accounts.

A Picture for Perspective

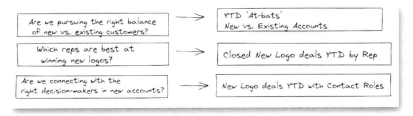

You can add value for functional leaders who aren't Salesforce experts by helping connect the dots between questions about their business and specific reports that can illuminate the information they need.

Pro tip: When building dashboards and reports, incorporate questions in your report titles or dashboard headers or subheaders to clarify the insight each widget will provide. For instance, instead of "Meetings by Account type" as the header on your dashboard chart, use that as the subhead with a title like "Are we meeting with enough new accounts?" If the team has a quota for the number of meetings they schedule, include that, too, and use conditional formatting to highlight who is and is not hitting it.

Sample Scenario 2

"Why are my reps losing deals, and what should I do about it?"

Let's go back to the scenario with Ritika, the sales leader looking for insight on why there were so many lost deals. She asked for a new field to assess where her team was losing deals in the sales cycle.

When you meet with her, you first pull up an Opportunity record and point out the opportunity stage history. You then run an Opportunity History report, demonstrating that the results can be summarized by the From or To stage.

"Who knew?" she says, adding that she's spent years looking at the stage changes on the Opportunity record, never realizing that it was reportable.

Next, you say, "It sounds like you're worried that your team is losing too many deals. How do you measure that?"

She understands each rep's overall performance but admits she doesn't regularly monitor win-loss percentages.

You take the action item to build her a dashboard based on win-loss reports, including metrics that will make it easy to understand win-loss ratios in various ways. For instance, you will create components to show win-loss percentages by rep based on both deal quantity and dollar value across multiple factors such as deal size, account type, and From stage.

Before you wrap up the meeting, you ask: "Ritika, since the impetus for our meeting was your concern about the number of deals your team is losing, I'm curious what processes are in place to facilitate follow-up on lost opportunities?"

She shares that they don't have structure around this and asks what you have in mind.

You offer a couple of ideas:

- **Implement a lost opportunity contest** to incent reps to reach out to all deals lost within the past 12 months, including a dashboard to display progress by rep and email templates to standardize communication.

- **Use automation** to institutionalize a follow-up process after a deal is lost, such as automatically sending emails to key contacts at specific intervals and auto-assigning tasks to reps to check in with the account.

- **Implement a flow** to send a thank-you note and survey link to the prospect to uncover more about their buying decision.

- **Use a Chatter group, Quip, or Slack** to set up a "How to win back lost deals" discussion in which reps can get resources, ask questions, and share experiences specific to the campaign.

"Wow! You've given me a lot to think about," says Ritika. "These are excellent ideas I'd like to share with my counterparts to consider how we might incorporate them consistently across the regions."

Well done! You've applied your Salesforce expertise to not only help Ritika uncover insights but provide actionable examples of how Salesforce can help her team win more deals and recover lost opportunities. Do you hear that noise? It's the sound of your points ratcheting up on the value-o-meter!

Turn Insight into Action

Illuminating available data is only half the fun. What's impactful is when you can help your business partners creatively leverage the Salesforce platform to act on the knowledge they glean. With your help, your leaders can better understand what's happening, and then you can use your Salesforce admin acumen to find ways to address the issue.

Here's the problem. Here's how I can help you solve it. Boom. This is how you get a seat at the table.

Suppose Laura, the sales manager concerned about the low number of new logo deals, drills into the data and sees that her sales reps are getting qualified leads in net-new accounts but are only selling to one contact in the prospect company. She knows this is a recipe for lost deals, but how can Salesforce help?

Or maybe Ritika determines that the reps regularly losing sales before they get a chance to bid aren't following their prescribed sales training process.

For these problems, you might suggest numerous solutions. Keep in mind that there's no single right answer. Some features are likely already used in your organization but not garnering the management attention they deserve. You can score some wins by pointing out these things to your team leads or creating reports and dashboards for improved tracking. There are likely also some net-new ways to apply Salesforce capabilities to the issue at hand. Your goal is to ensure that your team leaders know everything the platform offers and help them connect the dots on how features could solve their problems.

Let's look at a few examples in the sales arena.

Problem: Sales reps aren't spending enough time on the right deals.

Possible solution: Leverage Einstein Opportunity Scoring to identify deals that warrant more attention, specifically deals in the late stages with low scores and those in the early stages with high scores.

Problem: Sales reps aren't following the prescribed sales process.

Possible solution: Update the path in the Opportunity record to indicate which actions reps should take during each deal stage, and include links to training materials for each. Consider whether you need to adjust the validation rules or use other Salesforce admin sorcery to enforce critical steps for each deal stage.

Problem: Reps aren't identifying or engaging with all decision makers during the sales process.

Possible solution: Introduce Contact Roles to see if the reps are selling at a high enough level and if they're identifying and interacting with all the different influencers (for example, gatekeeper, procurement, and technical reviewer). Create reports and dashboards to help your leadership team bake the concept into their management practices. Hint: Don't forget to customize the values for the different roles that are most common in your organization.

Problem: Reps are repeatedly pushing out close dates and missing their forecasts.

Possible solution: Activate Pipeline Inspection so sales managers have better visibility into the opportunities in the pipeline. Sales Managers can quickly identify deals that have had amounts reduced, close dates pushed out, or other red flags that could indicate a coaching opportunity, such as the Next Steps field not being updated in more than seven days.

The Sales Cloud sweet spot is improving sales results, so I'm barely scratching the surface with these examples. What additional solutions can you come up with for each of these challenges? Do you see how these conversations can create value for your stakeholders and elevate your reputation as a business partner?

Sample Scenario 3

"How will this new program impact my customer service agents?"

The previous examples were Sales Cloud–centric, but you can employ this technique with any part of the platform. Suppose you work on the Service Cloud, and Akiko, who runs the call center, asks if you could add some new charts to her team performance dashboard. Her request is straightforward, so you could just update the reports and dashboard and send her a note when it's complete, asking her to let you know if she needs any tweaks or changes.

Instead, you pick up the phone to see what prompted this request.

As you chat, she discloses that her team has a new directive related to a program the company is rolling out for existing customers. The agents will need to ask a few additional questions as part of the case resolution process and take corresponding follow-up steps based on the answers. She is concerned that this will add significant time to resolution and cause confusion for the agents. Several of them are already struggling with all the steps required for the case resolution process.

You realize that the reports Akiko wants will help her assess if and how the new program impacts her team, but they won't address the root cause. You can provide her with a killer dashboard that can illuminate the bottlenecks and the impact of the process change on the team, but creating value will mean going a step further to suggest solutions based on that insight.

Service Cloud provides endless possibilities for improving the customer support process, so you spend additional time with Akiko to explore options to address her underlying concern. Potential actions to streamline her team's workflow include:

- Set up the Lightning Service Console app to increase agent efficiency

- Present a flow screen to walk agents through a dynamic script

- Configure a Salesforce quick action, flow, or macro to perform all sorts of "automagic" to reduce the team's clicks

- Implement Live Agent or an Einstein bot to reduce the need for agent interaction

Hoorah! Instead of being an order taker, you've applied your business analysis skills and platform expertise to generate ideas to improve the team's efficiency and effectiveness. Akiko's request for a dashboard was the jumping-off point for discussion, not just an order to be filled. You leveraged a simple request to uncover areas where you could meld your understanding of the problem with your platform knowledge to deliver serious value to your stakeholders.

CAUTION! A CALM-THE-CHAOS CAVEAT

I have one colossal caveat, given that this book is about creating value *and* erecting guardrails to prevent overwhelm. The act of enlightening your stakeholders with the art of the possible does *not* equate to a commitment to dropping everything and immediately implementing your suggestions. Talking about how your leaders can better leverage the platform is not the same as committing to do the work.

Ideally, some of their requests will fall in the quick-hit category, such that you can provide some immediate value. But if you don't have the bandwidth to engage, you can still have the conversation but preface it accordingly. If specific ideas resonate, set the expectation that they will be prioritized in your intake process, just as any other request.

Pro tip: Some ideas you raise may require substantial effort or incremental costs, and you must set expectations accordingly. Part of providing expert advice is ensuring that your constituents have a realistic understanding of the effort and resources required, including your time and theirs. If there's an interest in moving forward, but the work will impact your other commitments, discuss trade-offs early and often. Ask your stakeholders to articulate the value and priority of any proposed workstream. Then partner with them to create a business case that includes adequate resourcing for initial development and ongoing support.

Pro tip: Be mindful of the cumulative impact of adding new features, functionality, and user groups, including minor business as usual (BAU) enhancements. Individually, these small changes might not warrant a discussion about resource requirements for ongoing support, but their collective impact can quickly add up. Even if features are easy to implement, they still increase the number of things you need to monitor, maintain, and inevitably iterate over time. Reviewing the cumulative impact of system enhancements should be an ongoing discussion with your manager and your Salesforce steering committee.

TALK TRACKS:

Setting Stakeholder Expectations

➢ Given that you're getting ready to start your campaign and my plate is full, I can't offer any help with this one. Still, I'd love to talk to you about a few ideas you may want to consider the next time you have a similar initiative.

➢ Once you and the other regional leaders kick around these ideas, I'd like to understand which ones will have the most impact so we can prioritize and develop a phased approach.

➢ The ideas we've discussed will require additional licenses to the tune of $25K annually and a significant investment of time from your team during the design and deployment process. Given that, what's your interest level in moving forward?

➢ What would be the impact of each of the ideas we discussed? I'll need to reshuffle commitments if this work gets prioritized, so I'll need your help articulating the business case.

CHAPTER 6:

PROVIDE CONTEXT

Taken out of context I must seem so strange.

—Ani DiFranco

We've covered the importance of understanding the context behind questions and requests for solutions. It's equally important to *proactively provide* the appropriate context when communicating with your stakeholders to align expectations and ensure they understand the implications when considering an approach or design decision.

From a Salesforce perspective, this means you may want to provide some baseline information to help your constituents understand the process by which the platform gets customized and how that might differ from other technology solutions. This context is essential when dealing with stakeholders new to Salesforce and those whose previous technology encounters were limited to old-school on-premises software or complex custom development. Likewise, your business partners should understand the art of the possible and have a sense of what is and is not easy on the platform to help inform the decisions you will make together. Providing context around how things work—and, more importantly, what this means regarding how you'll work with them—will lead to better collaboration.

Show Them What's Behind the Curtain

As a general rule, your constituents have no idea what's involved in setting up a new Salesforce system or making changes to their existing platform applications. Stakeholders new to the platform or who weren't closely involved in the original build likely won't have any context about software-as-a-service applications and the benefits they provide. They may only know the challenges of working with traditional software or a homegrown application, which could lead to misunderstandings and tension in the deployment process. The goal is not to overwhelm them with technical terms or train up an army of Salesforce admins in your business units but to provide enough context to set expectations, generate excitement, and reduce unnecessary friction.

Suppose you are extending the use of Salesforce to a new business unit that has been working on a homegrown application rife with clunky workarounds and field labels that don't match the current business process. For years they've been told that they have to make it work, as it would be difficult and costly to upgrade or change. Some team members still remember and complain about how long it took to build it in the first place. They may harbor a grudge about the hours they spent describing their needs to the software team and still ending up with something that didn't quite fit the bill, and they couldn't get funds to make additional changes. You can imagine that this team will likely have various preconceived ideas that could impact your project's success unless you provide some context and adjust expectations.

Based on how they experienced technology projects in the past, you may find that they want to put on paper everything they can think of that they might *ever* need the system to do, from soup to nuts, believing they have only one shot to get their needs met. This can slow you down and cause friction as they try to solve for every possible what-if scenario or debate for hours on the perfect field label.

For instance, you may be planning a high-level discussion regarding which data points need to be available for reporting, which is critical to ensure that you capture all the necessary data. During the early stage of the project, you won't dive into the nitty-gritty report details, such as which fields to display and in what order, as that's easy stuff you can adjust with Report Builder once you're ready to set up some reports.

However, the reality for your constituents may have been that changes to internal applications, including report requirements, necessitate an Act of Congress. Their previous system may have required special software packages for reporting and specialists who run database queries. If this is their expectation, they may feel frustrated or concerned that you aren't asking enough questions about their reporting needs early in the process.

Show Them What You Mean by Easy Breezy

Before discussing a future-state business process or desired outcome for a significant initiative, if you're working with a team unfamiliar with Salesforce, provide a brief backstage tour. You can add value from the get-go by helping them understand that they aren't in Kansas anymore, including revealing a few of your declarative admin tricks. You don't need to teach them how to do it, just give them the context that Salesforce works differently than systems they've used in the past.

Level setting these concepts can alleviate problems before they begin. Demonstrate things that will help them understand Salesforce configuration capabilities to get them excited about the project and its benefits. This perspective should help them be more specific about their requirements when you start having those conversations. After all, imagine the response you would get if you asked someone who's never seen a smartphone which apps they want and in what order on the screen.

- **Custom fields:** Demonstrate that right before their very eyes, a Salesforce admin can add a field and make it immediately available for reporting in just a few clicks; no code or army of programmers required.

- **Page layouts:** Edit a page layout to demonstrate how quickly you can add sections, rearrange fields, add related lists, configure the highlights panel, and do other magic.

- **Dashboards:** Assuming you have another team using dashboards for a similar use case, show that. Otherwise, pick any dashboard and show them how you can drill down into a particular report to a specific record in just a few clicks. Show them how easy it is to reorder dashboard widgets and change component types.

- **Report Builder:** Start with a tabular report and show how users can slice and dice it using standard features to summarize the data, drill down to a subset, or change the date range. Open Report Builder and show them you can add fields, rearrange columns, and adjust the filter criteria. Let them know that all the fields you add for them will be reportable.

- **Sharing and security:** If you're working with a team that needs to capture sensitive data, consider demonstrating how you can configure and restrict sharing at the object, record, and field levels.

- **Salesforce Mobile:** If mobile is in scope, show them how they'll work with identical records in a browser or the mobile app. Demonstrate how you can create mobile layouts to optimize the user experience on a smaller device.

Providing this type of information to your stakeholders has several advantages:

- **They will begin to understand what's possible** and how the system will benefit them, reducing apprehension about change.

- **They'll have more accurate expectations** regarding how you'll conduct discovery meetings. They'll understand the types of questions you'll ask and why there may be some seemingly critical questions you *won't* ask until you get closer to the go-live date.

- **They'll understand what types of tweaks are reasonable to request.** As a proactive Salesforce admin extraordinaire, you want to uncover what's working and not working, scenarios and edge cases that might have been overlooked, and small changes that could benefit users. Obtaining this information, either as feedback or as the outcome of deskside sessions with your users, is how you continually improve the system and delight the teams using it.

CAUTION! A CALM-THE-CHAOS CAVEAT

There's value in sharing the simplicity of configuring on the Salesforce platform, but it's equally important to set expectations that enhancement requests won't be immediately implemented. Based on your consistent delivery of value-adding features and functionality, your constituents will come to believe that a little Salesforce pixie dust is all it takes to automate a new process, complete with a shiny dashboard with a cherry on top. In the real world, however, Salesforce admin feats take time—or at least uninterrupted mindshare—and require governance before you start making system changes. You'll want to communicate that just because they saw you add a field in minutes doesn't mean you'll do that on the fly in production or immediately deliver all enhancement requests. Share the process for intaking and prioritizing changes and ensure they understand that additional steps are required for deployment, including testing, updating documentation, and migrating across multiple sandbox environments.

Explain What's Not Easy Breezy

It is also helpful to communicate that certain things that seem surprisingly easy will have tangles or be impossible without heavy lifting, and some requests may be feasible but will require code. Providing context ensures stakeholders understand the implications, such as longer development time and much less flexibility regarding future changes.

When working through requirements with my stakeholders, I indicate what's easy, what falls in the "complex config" category, and what requires code. This is a helpful way to frame a discussion about the trade-off of reduced complexity in return for more flexibility and faster value (which we'll cover in the next chapter). Given the pace of change these days, stakeholders will frequently deprioritize nice-to-haves in exchange for a quicker, more flexible solution.

A Real-Life Example: Context Matters

Years ago, as part of a global Salesforce deployment, I took a gig leading in-person training sessions. I joined the team as the project was going live, so I wasn't involved in setting up the system. The key project sponsors had never worked with Salesforce and were accustomed to more traditional software projects with more rigid design sign-offs.

After several training sessions, it became evident that a few critical concepts in their lead process required a great deal of explanation. The sales reps repeatedly interrupted with questions, preventing us from getting through the material. I approached the project executive and explained the situation, recommending a simple solution to add field-level help text with the instructions and definitions applicable to the fields generating the questions. I explained how this would improve ongoing usability and data quality and serve as quick reference material during the sessions.

"Yes. I get why that would be helpful, and I wish we had thought about that before," she said. "Unfortunately, we have signed off on the design and agreed to no further changes. We'll have to consider that as requirements for Phase 2, which we plan to start next quarter."

"So, by any chance, have you seen the process for adding help text?"

As I asked the question, I cracked open my laptop, logged into a sandbox, navigated to the set-up screen, and typed some sample text. I then pulled up a Lead record to show that I could "hover to discover" to see the text I'd just added.

Nobody on the project had provided any context about which things were easy to change. I'm referring to minor changes that are expected and recommended to translate early learnings into quick improvements.

Granted, there are times when a significant amount of work has been done on training videos or other learning aids such that even minor adjustments to the system would require substantial effort. In these instances, it makes sense to explore whether the benefit of the change warrants the rework or the change is minor enough that it doesn't require updating the materials.

In this case, the project sponsor had no idea that just-in-time iterations were even possible until I showed her. She immediately recognized the benefit and signed off on the changes. Sure enough, these minor tweaks resulted in fewer training-session questions, allowing us time to get through all the essential materials and improve the sales team's overall user experience.

 ## TALK TRACKS:

Providing Context about the Solution

➢ Most of what I'm hearing are things we can accomplish quickly, whereas a few things you've mentioned will add a lot of complexity. Can we drill into these requirements to determine if they warrant the work and explore whether there are opportunities to simplify in exchange for a more flexible, faster solution?

➢ If I told you that accounting for that edge case would add at least a week to the project timeline due to the added complexity, would you still want to include it?

➢ Is that requirement a must-have or a nice-to-have? I'm asking because that will require a developer to write code, adding complexity now and when you need to make changes.

➢ So far, all the changes you've asked for are very simple. As your team starts working in the system, please keep this type of feedback coming, as that's how we'll continue to improve it. I can't commit to implementing all the asks immediately, but we'll get them evaluated and prioritized.

Pro tip: If you have the good fortune of having project resources such as business analysts or project managers assigned to your workstreams, ensure that these team members understand how Salesforce works. Without this context, BAs may over-rotate when documenting requirements, such as listing every field needed in a report or the specific order for every field on the page layout. Project managers may be overly stringent on code-freeze deadlines or unwilling to allow even the smallest configuration change without shifting the project schedule. Help them understand the effort required for system changes and differentiate between things that need detailed documentation versus list views and basic reports that you can configure in a more ad-hoc manner with input from your stakeholders.

Pro tip: Your boss may also require some Salesforce context, particularly if you report to someone with no experience as a Salesforce practitioner. If you're doing your job well, your boss is probably very aware of your value but unaware of the effort you expend to make it happen. They may not appreciate why certain things take so long. Ensure your boss understands precisely what's involved with keeping the lights on and all the projects and initiatives you're completing. One way to do this is to use a ticketing system, which allows you to report on your completed work and backlog items and provide context on the volume and variation of the work in your queue. We'll discuss ticketing systems in Chapter 11.

CHAPTER 7:

TAKE A PAGE FROM PRODUCT MANAGEMENT

It's really hard to design products by focus groups. A lot of times, people don't know what they want until you show it to them.

—Steve Jobs

So far, we've discussed the importance of putting on your BA hat to get to the heart of the business requirements and the why behind the request. We've looked at ways to provide expert advice as part of the solutions you deliver and guidance you share, including the importance of providing context. This chapter examines specific ways to create value by taking a page from the product management playbook. Yep, product manager is yet another hat you'll wear!

First, if you're unfamiliar with this discipline, I'll define it and its relation to your role as Salesforce admin. Then we'll explore how borrowing a few fundamental product management principles can elevate your Salesforce admin game.

What's Product Management and What Does it Have to Do with You?

Much as it's hard to nail down a single definition of Salesforce admin given how the role differs across companies, product manager can be an equally varied role. It is quite prevalent in the software industry. Product managers typically partner with the Engineering and Design teams to translate business needs and the company vision into a tactical plan that delivers value. They help uncover and prioritize the problems that need to be solved. In conjunction with stakeholders and engineers, they help define solutions. Their role is to delight customers and keep stakeholders happy. Does this sound similar to the type of work you do?

Key product management activities include:

1. Establishing the product vision and roadmap

2. Prioritizing enhancements, including discussing trade-offs and aligning on what will and won't get done in the time frame

3. Ensuring that the business process is fully defined before engaging Engineering

4. Demoing early and often

5. Shipping quickly ("Shipping product" is a term rarely used in the software-as-a-service space. Our version is delivering rapid value with fast and frequent deployments, often referred to as speed to value.)

Although the product management discipline may be new to you, I'm willing to bet that you see overlap with your role.

Salesforce's meteoric rise was fueled in part by the "No Software" tagline. For years, before Salesforce matured into an enterprise platform, functional business teams intentionally implemented Salesforce with little or no assistance from the IT department. This notion of Salesforce as the antithesis to all things software may explain why the Salesforce ecosystem has been slow to adopt this discipline, a staple in the digital space.

As the platform becomes increasingly complex, we need to own up to the fact that we are developing software, even if it involves clicks instead of code. The increase in capabilities and complexity on the platform likely explains why we're now hearing more product management vernacular in the Salesforce community and seeing more job postings for Salesforce product roles. I suspect this is a growing trend, so it's a great time to break in your product manager hat.

Embrace an Agile Mindset

These days, you would be hard-pressed to read anything about product management that doesn't assume or prescribe software development using Agile principles. If you're not familiar with the term, Agile is an iterative and incremental approach in which teams work through a series of time-boxed "sprints" that result in having defined pieces of work completed and ready to be released to users. The objective is to collaborate closely with everyone involved, deliver quickly, learn from the process, and iterate accordingly.

Agile has almost universally replaced the Waterfall method, in which the project team documents every requirement before all features are coded and deployed in somewhat of a big-bang approach. With traditional software projects, design changes are complicated and costly. The advantage of Waterfall is that it gets the business team and engineers to agree on every requirement before writing code to reduce the need for expensive and time-consuming code changes. The disadvantage is that it's tough to go back and make changes for missed requirements or processes that weren't entirely thought through or understood.

Because of its declarative capabilities, Salesforce inherently lends itself to an agile, iterative process. The beauty of Salesforce and our clicks-not-code wizardry is that we can build things quickly and then iterate as needed. It's in our DNA. But regardless of your familiarity with Agile, appropriating a few key tenets and being "Agile-ish" will enable you to deliver speed to value and frequently "ship product" that wows your stakeholders.

Demo Early and Often

A key goal of all good product managers is having something ready to show as quickly as possible to elicit early feedback. Speed is also a Salesforce sweet spot. And we have a built-in advantage. Traditional software development has to rely on wireframes to illustrate a prototype or design concept. We get to spin up a dev org and bring things to life. It's why Salesforce's sales teams can wow prospective customers when they show up with a demo that already looks and feels like what the customer needs.

When designing Salesforce solutions, we can sketch a data model and then quickly mock up a proposed solution to have something tangible to show our stakeholders. The intent is not to have a fully functioning feature but a first cut to provoke discussion. Plus, getting hands on keyboards as quickly as possible is the best way to figure out the right solution, where there are potential gotchas, and what additional information you need from the business team. For those of us who think with our hands and dream in custom objects, diving deep into a dev org to start contemplating how to solve the business problem is where the magic happens.

Work toward getting something to show as soon as possible. Most people need to see something, and sometimes even play with it, before fully wrapping their heads around how a new process will work or identifying design flaws. Before spending time on process automation, show some basic screens and discuss how you envision the process will work.

I'm always amazed by how much faster we can firm up business requirements and agree on a solution when we have something demonstratable the team can react to instead of having a hypothetical conversation or a drawing on a whiteboard. You don't need to add every single field or set up any automation. That should wait until you've agreed on an approach, but enabling the business team to see a data model that resembles their business process allows you to confirm you're on the right path, eliminating rework and increasing project velocity. Ensuring alignment is particularly important when solutioning something that may look different from the specific request, as discussed in the preceding chapters.

In the scenario with Gwen, the communication manager who worked with franchisees, as soon as she saw the new Certification object, she not only understood the proposed solution and its advantages, she got excited. You made a fan! She might have had a different reaction, possibly adverse or at least less enthusiastic, had you not shown her the solution and instead tried to describe it with words like "custom object" and "master-detail relationship," which would likely have been meaningless to her.

Set the expectation that you'll plan a series of short, frequent demo sessions as you continue to iterate and refine the solution. When conducting a demo, provide your audience a few minutes to digest what they see. Then use your questioning skills to make sure you're on the right track and elicit feedback on how you can make it better. Often, you will get new requirements and changes to the original request as they see the solution in action. Making iterative changes during the design process is not a bad thing. This collaboration is how you create solutions that knock people's socks off.

 ## TALK TRACKS:

Confirming Alignment on the Solution

➤ Are we on track?

➤ What do you think?

➤ Is that what you were hoping to see?

➤ How does this compare to what you were envisioning?

➤ Where are the gaps?

➤ What's missing?

➤ What do you like best?

➤ Is there anything missing that would increase value?

DOS AND DON'TS FOR DEMOS

- **Do** work on having something ready to show as soon as possible.

- **Do** prepopulate sample records to provide a realistic picture of the solution.

- **Do** have a script you'll walk them through, ideally in the form of a scenario that looks and feels like their business process.

- **Do** point out any bonus features you added to confirm that they meet their needs and rack up some extra credit.

- **Do** use the demo as an opportunity to point out tips and tricks.

- **Do** get confirmation that you're on target.

- **Do** be on guard for requests that come out of left field, as imaginations tend to go wild once people see the power of the platform. Have questions such as "Help me understand how this ties back to our immediate objective" handy. If requests don't fit or add complexity, put them in the backlog.

- **Don't** spend too much time on a configuration before confirming that you're on the right track. Anything complex should wait until you and your stakeholders agree on the approach.

Deliver Small Chunks and Iterate

A core concept in the product management world that fits well with an agile, iterative approach is that of the MVP, minimum viable product. (As an aside, this is an example where Salesforce vernacular doesn't align with the product management discipline. In the Salesforce Ohana, we use the phrase the same way it's often used in sports to celebrate our most valuable professionals, whom we recognize for their contributions to the Salesforce community.) For product managers, MVP means developing and deploying the lowest level of product sophistication to meet the business need, allowing you to deliver value as quickly as possible to stakeholders and then iterating and enhancing in subsequent release cycles. It means not overcomplicating a solution right out of the gate. Deploy version 1.0 before you add every conceivable bell and whistle. Get something built and into production so teams can start using it, providing a much faster time to value and feedback that will yield incremental improvement.

The MVP approach is a perfect fit for the value-adding Salesforce admin. It falls right in our wheelhouse in terms of delivering quick wins and speed to value. If you can align your stakeholders around the MVP concept, you'll reduce risks, including the likelihood of deploying extraneous features and functionality that no one will use. As a rule of thumb, the more robust a release, the more chance for errors and the so-called Law of Unintended Consequences.

The concept of deploying MVP is even more critical when automating a net-new business process. In this case, work with your business partner to determine the bare minimum to get started. Even if they swear that their new process is fully baked, inevitably there will be tons of tweaks and changes required as teams start doing whatever function you are facilitating on the platform.

The more features you include in the first version, the more things you will inevitably have to change. Shortly after the launch date, you'll often hear comments like "It never occurred to me that the team would use it like that." Or "It turns out that filling out the fields in that section is more trouble than it's worth." And then there's the ever-popular "Now that we're using this, we realized that what we *really* need is…"

Have you heard anything like this after you deployed a change or helped automate a new business process? If so, don't worry. It's not because you missed critical requirements during the discovery session. Our stakeholders often can't comprehend all the nuances regarding how a new Salesforce-powered business process will work or conceive of every possible edge case and downstream impact until they start using it. In the next section, I'll discuss preparing for the inevitable change requests you'll get after go-live, including setting stakeholder expectations accordingly with something I call the warranty period.

Your business partners may be resistant to an MVP approach. Their resistance might stem from the fact that their previous technology experience was comprised entirely of Waterfall projects, so they are accustomed to big-bang deployments. They may have concerns about incremental releases because multiple communications or training sessions will be required. You can counter these concerns by discussing the impact of the change. Your users can only absorb so much newness at once. Introducing new features in bite-sized chunks makes it easier for them to digest, and they'll be more likely to retain the knowledge and use the new functionality.

Your stakeholders also may be skeptical that they'll get another bite at the apple. You say it will be an incremental, iterative approach, but their experience may be that a new priority comes up once Version 1.0 is live and Version 2.0 never materializes. Sometimes the resistance to incremental deployments may stem from the fact that they are impatient, excited, or simply demanding and want it all at once. (I'm sure you don't have stakeholders like that, right?) It is helpful to discuss the benefits of faster time to value and risk mitigation, but it sometimes takes a few real-world proof points.

CAUTION! A CALM-THE-CHAOS CAVEAT

An MVP approach must not translate into delivering incomplete solutions or features that aren't comprehensive enough to provide value. For this reason, you'll sometimes hear people refer to the concept of a minimum *lovable* product. Even though you will continue to iterate and improve, you still need to meet business outcomes and make your users productive immediately.

TALK TRACKS:

Aligning on MVP

➤ We can meet the basics to support this new process in a short time frame, but those extra bells and whistles will add tremendous complexity. Since those aren't critical to the process, I propose that our first release exclude those. Once we implement this, we can plan a fast-follow release if you feel that's the right next priority. How does that sound?

➤ We've talked about different ideas. Let's pick one and get it implemented before we tackle the rest. I'd recommend starting with this one. What do you think?

➤ Once we decommission that system, there's a lot we can do to improve the process. I recommend deploying the minimum functionality needed to transition into Salesforce, and then we can continue to iterate and add new features. How do you feel about that approach?

Pro tip: Often, you won't know until you start building the solution that certain aspects of the request are particularly complex or time-consuming. If it turns out that specific components are overly complicated or have more tangles than expected, provide some context to explain why those components are time-consuming and ask your stakeholders whether the effort is warranted. If the complex elements are required, you can add them in an incremental release or negotiate more time or resources to account for the unexpected effort.

CHAPTER 8:

SOLVE PROBLEMS, EVEN ONES THEY DON'T KNOW THEY HAVE

Problems are nothing but wake-up calls for creativity.

—Gerhard Gschwandtner

We've covered numerous scenarios illustrating that problem solver is yet another hat worn by Salesforce admins. Solving problems is inherent in the job description. It defines what you do each time you listen to your constituents and then tweak, configure, and deploy solutions. They share their business problems, often requiring open-ended questions and a decoder ring to get to the heart of the matter. You combine critical thinking, creativity, and Salesforce ninja skills to bring a solution to life. Problem solved. But, as they say in the advertising world, "Wait, there's more!"

In addition to reacting to issues your stakeholders raise, you can compound your value by leveraging your vantage point to proactively identify challenges and recommend system and process improvements. Between the insights you glean from wrangling users and data all day and your perspective from working across multiple teams, you're well-positioned to spot areas needing a slight tune-up or complete overhaul. Taking the initiative to identify and address issues demonstrates your ownership mindset. The ability to uncover and resolve significant, more strategic challenges and the nitty-gritty issues that vex your users demonstrates your agility and elevates your value. You can cover considerable ground, growing your fan base across many types of constituents when you're comfortable and capable at both the 30,000-foot macro level and down in the weeds.

This chapter provides specific ways to use your unique viewpoint to recognize and resolve process problems, system challenges, and other issues your peeps may not even know they have.

Facilitate the View from Above

Most Salesforce admins deal with numerous intersecting business teams such as Marketing, Sales, and Customer Service. If you're in this category, you likely have a more holistic view of the end-to-end business process than the individuals that work within those teams. You may be privy to all sorts of information they don't have, allowing you to provide expert advice when teams surface new initiatives. You're also likely to have insight into bottlenecks, redundancies, and existing procedures that could use a little reengineering. You have the opportunity to observe business processes that are missing, broken, or otherwise flawed. In some cases, your business partners may not be aware of the problem, as they only look at their piece of the puzzle. In other cases, they may never have raised the issue because they weren't aware there was an easy solution or "It's always been done this way."

Because most companies' business units are more siloed than they want to admit, your view across multiple teams or departments means you may have better evidence about why a particular path forward is or is not a good idea. Your stakeholders may be busy, myopic, or both and may not necessarily understand cross-department issues or processes. Clarifying the impacts or raising discussion topics that might otherwise not be addressed and bringing diverse groups to a common understanding is a valuable service you may be uniquely positioned to provide.

A Real-Life Example

Years ago, I took a Salesforce job supporting a global sales team. As I got to know the org, I learned that they weren't using the Lead object and that the sales reps didn't have the system permission to create new Account records. When a rep wanted to start calling on a company that wasn't already in the Salesforce database, they had to request the Credit team conduct a credit inquiry by submitting a form hosted on the intranet.

It took a day or two for the team to approve the company's credit and then communicate to the Salesforce admin, who would enter the Account record. Meanwhile, reps were having calls and meetings they weren't tracking in Salesforce or, even worse, holding off on contacting potentially hot leads. The Credit team was expending energy before there was even a deal to pursue, let alone one qualified enough to warrant their involvement.

Anyone tasked with ensuring data integrity would agree that it makes sense to have controls regarding new Account creation, but this seemed counterproductive, so I started digging in.

My working hypothesis was that we should implement the Leads functionality so the sales reps would have a place to track their initial activity and could use the integrated tools to do some basic company research before initiating the credit inquiry. I figured I could streamline getting the information to the Credit team by creating some sort of dynamic link, screen flow, or "easy button" that would pass the required fields into the web form so the reps could initiate the process from the Lead record. Of course, I also intended to explore moving the Credit team's workflow into Salesforce.

The more I dug to confirm my initial assumptions, the more flaws I found in the logic behind the entire process. The Marketing team would periodically upload lists, creating hundreds or even thousands of new Account records. If those happened to be the companies the rep wanted to call on, they could proceed without a credit check. Plus, thousands of existing companies were in the system that either had never had a credit check or hadn't had one in a very long time. Reps were able to add Opportunity records to these without a credit inquiry. If the purpose was to ensure that reps were only spending time with financially stable companies, this was not happening for a significant number of deals in the pipeline.

The Credit team didn't see the macro-level picture to understand how many prospects the sales team was engaging without their involvement or how many companies had a credit inquiry but never had a qualified opportunity. They were so busy executing all the credit checks that they didn't have time to come up for air to consider the process implications. The sales leadership team hadn't bothered to dig into the details to understand the problem. They heard their reps complain that it was hard to get Account records created and assumed they were just making excuses to avoid using Salesforce or justify a sparse pipeline.

Once I outlined the gaps and how the process negatively impacted the early-stage sales cycle, all key stakeholders recognized that this credit inquiry step was unnecessary and agreed to eliminate it. Instead, we automated a credit check further along in the sales cycle.

I share this story to illustrate how having a broad, cross-functional perspective can uncover process inefficiencies and solve problems that teams may not even acknowledge as issues. The intent is not to take a red pen and draw frowny faces on all existing process maps but to take a step back and see where it might make sense to streamline how teams work together or reimagine a more straightforward process. Sometimes our value add doesn't have anything to do with enhancing Salesforce. Because we see the bigger picture, we can score some wins by facilitating discussions, identifying process breakdowns, and eliminating wasted work.

Communicate Possibilities Even Though "It's Always Been Done This Way"

Psychologists use the term "status quo bias" to describe an emotional preference for the current situation. In short, people don't like change even when it would make things better. It's difficult, it takes work, and there's uncertainty.

Salesforce admins frequently face pushback from users resistant to adopting a new system or business partners reluctant to raise their hand to surface issues that might require change. "We've always done it this way" can be a challenging refrain to overcome, but you can prevail by identifying an improved approach or a better solution. By leveraging your curiosity and business analyst skills, you will uncover processes that are redundant, suboptimal, or no longer needed. Take the time to validate your assumptions, gain consensus, and demonstrate the benefit of the change to ensure that each team understands what's in it for them. You'll inevitably find that your constituents will willingly get on board when you can save them time or clicks and make them more efficient.

Platform Enhancements Enable Process Improvements

If you work in a Salesforce org that is more than a few years old, you'll find numerous opportunities for improvement without needing to look too hard. System and process changes seldom keep pace with all the enhancements in Salesforce seasonal releases. Many things are possible using declarative customizations that probably weren't possible years ago when your company first deployed Salesforce or automated a particular process. Back then, specific automation may have required boatloads of code and therefore been deemed not worth the effort. For example, somewhere in your Salesforce system, it's likely users are unnecessarily creating records manually because that would have required a ton of code to automate back in the day.

Now you can point and click to make the magic happen. Additionally, certain features may not have been as robust as they are today. Seasonal releases are chock full of goodies you can employ to enhance your system and grow your fan base.

Here are a few platform improvements that may yield easy wins:

- Identify where quick actions can reduce clicks needed to create new records or complete specific tasks.

- Activate the setting that allows users to add Account records as campaign members and get rave reviews from sales teams that do account-based marketing.

- Revisit the Contact Role and Opportunity Product objects. Both have both had upgrades and now operate more like other standard objects. If you manage Sales Cloud, there's a good chance the ability to run automation from a Contact Role record or create a lookup relationship with the Opportunity Product object might scratch an itch that's been around for a while.

- Activate the setting to control which objects are included in Einstein Search and customize it for each user profile. (This can be a win if you regularly field calls from users telling you their records are missing because the object they're searching for isn't displayed in the search results. Serve up what your users need to see in search instead of repeatedly showing how to click "More" to see additional objects.)

- Get creative with Flow Builder to present dynamic screens and reduce manual steps. After all, what *can't* you do with a flow these days?

A Real-Life Example: Report Distribution No Longer Requires Manual Intervention

On one engagement, I met a Salesforce admin who had time scheduled on his calendar every Friday to export and then email several reports to a particular business group. Curious, I asked if there was a reason he couldn't automate this task. He explained that the reports had to be sent as Excel attachments. This requirement used to require code or a third-party application, but Salesforce now includes the ability to schedule reports with attachments, a huge time saver for Salesforce admins. After demonstrating this, I asked him what the recipients of the report data did with it. He admitted he had been doing it so long that he could no longer remember. I was interested in understanding the use case, so I asked him to loop back and let me know.

Sure enough, when he reached out, they told him they didn't need that information anymore. They had relied on it to support a commission program that had ended more than a year earlier.

Imagine the time saved if they had shared that information or if he'd been closer to the use case. Between an improvement in Salesforce functionality that could have automated this task and a requirement that was no longer needed, this Salesforce admin wasted many hours that he could have spent on value-adding activities.

Pro tip: A good place to identify quick wins resulting from platform enhancements is the User Interface page in the Platform Tools section in the Setup. Depending on the age of your org, there may be options that are no longer needed and settings that were added over time and never activated. Validate your assumptions and test any changes before you make them.

CAUTION! A CALM-THE-CHAOS CAVEAT

Problem-solving, proactive Salesforce admins are consultative, determine what their constituents need, and have the foresight to address problems, even those their constituents don't know they have. However, I encourage you to confirm your findings and validate your assumptions.

A Real-Life Example

Here's a cautionary tale about time spent on an assumption that wasn't validated. I worked for a company with a robust Sales Cloud implementation and was tasked with extending the Salesforce platform to the Procurement team. They needed a database to track their current and prospective vendors, including details such as primary contacts, insurance certificates, and contract renewal dates.

Great use of Salesforce, right? My team and I conducted a requirements meeting, asked plenty of questions, and sought to understand their use case. We planned to leverage the Account object, add a new record type, and tweak the sharing rules to ensure that vendor company records and any new fields added for this purpose were visible only to the Procurement team.

Easy! Being forward-thinking while we were building out this functionality, I was looking ahead at how I thought they would use the database once it was up and running. I was positive that the Procurement team would want to search by vendor subcategory. For example, "We need a company that does outsourcing or benefits consulting." Or "Show me all the approved IT vendors."

Easy that is, except for the inevitable gotcha. Based on how this team classified vendors, each vendor could be in multiple categories. Each could have numerous subcategories, which the team wanted to track in a multi-select picklist.

Grr! I'm sure you can relate to the frustration of having a data point that needs to be reported or searched but can't because it resides in a multi-select picklist!

No worries, I thought. I've got plenty of Salesforce admin tricks up my sleeve. I brainstormed all the ways to solve the problem, listing the pros and cons of each. We could use a flow to populate checkboxes behind the scenes based on the multi-select picklist's values or a junction object to create a one-to-many relationship between vendor and category. Heck, I could even ask our developers to whip up a custom Lightning component or some other code solution. The gears were spinning as I considered the best way to proceed and then mocked up a few options in the sandbox to get feedback. Meanwhile, tick-tock. I already had a full plate managing the Sales Cloud, and this was taking way more time than I'd anticipated when I told my boss I had the bandwidth for this project.

Here's the rub. When I met with the Procurement team and walked through the options to get their thoughts on the most intuitive approach, they stared blankly at me as if they didn't understand what problem I was trying to solve. It turned out that they had a limited group of approved vendors, so team members knew off the tops of their heads which vendors were approved in each category. They didn't need to search by category or subcategory and could not imagine any use case. It wasn't part of their business process.

The moral of this story is *not* that you should ignore tricky requirements and hope your users don't notice if there's a gap in what you deliver. Nor is it that you shouldn't think ahead to identify missed requirements or usability issues that will likely be apparent when the functionality gets deployed. Your knowledge of the platform and experience with how teams interact with the system are invaluable in weaving together a robust solution that exceeds stakeholder expectations. That's Salesforce admin gold! The point is to ensure you are not solutioning requirements that don't exist. When wearing your business analyst hat, determine which functionality they need beyond the specifics in their initial request, but confirm your findings before burning precious time and brain cells.

Earn Kudos for Solving Little Problems, Too

Problem solving doesn't have to be grandiose. Little things matter in terms of data quality, the user experience, and system adoption, so helping eliminate clicks or make it easier for users to navigate is also a big win. Over the years, I've learned that what's obvious to us as Salesforce admins is often not apparent to our users. Some of the sincerest thank yous I've received and the most profound aha moments I've witnessed resulted from merely sharing things that seemed incredibly self-evident but were not so obvious to people using the system.

TEN NOT-SO-OBVIOUS-AFTER-ALL QUICK WINS TO COMMUNICATE

- How to use relative date filters in reports and list views

- How to use inline editing in a report

- How to open a record in a different tab or window to avoid navigating away from a report or dashboard

- How to see a list view as a Kanban board

- How to hide or mute a Chatter feed

- How to "favorite" any record

- How to change the density on Lightning page layouts

- How to pin a list view

- How to use the standard dictation feature on a mobile device to update fields and enter text

- How to access valuable links and tools from the Lightning utility bar

Take the time to listen to your users' pain points and uncover their challenges, including scheduling SABWA sessions to watch how they navigate screens. The more you see how they interact with Salesforce, the more opportunities you'll have to share tips and tricks and solve many minor problems along the way.

Brainstorm New Ways to Solve Problems and New Problems to Solve

Ideas are a valuable currency. They're the spark that makes progress happen. Ideas will compound your ability to solve all sorts of business problems. We often get so busy in the day-to-day Salesforce admin weeds that we neglect to step back and apply our creativity to consider how and where we can make improvements. In my experience, every team huddle for a group brainstorm unearths something impactful that makes us wonder why we hadn't thought of it already and why we don't take time more often for a solid brainstorming session.

Ideas also demonstrate creativity and critical thinking. As I've helped numerous clients assess their Salesforce admin team's talent, one of the easiest ways to differentiate the extraordinary from the ordinary has been to engage them in a conversation about their ideas for improving their org. Enthusiastic Salesforce admins with an ownership mindset generally have dozens of ideas at the ready, running the gamut from system changes to process improvements they'd love to implement if they only had more time. Bringing ideas to the table is crucial for improving your system's quality, identifying areas for ongoing improvement, and creating value for your stakeholders.

Author and entrepreneur James Altucher has written several books and blogs about a method he uses to juice his creativity. He picks a topic and forces himself to generate ten new ideas daily to overcome perfectionism and build the "idea muscle" that gets creative juices flowing.[5]

Altucher recounts a tale about a manager who asked his team to come up with a great idea and, after a few minutes, no one had thought of anything. What if it wasn't the correct answer? What if the idea wasn't great?

He revised the request and asked them to come up with 20 ideas. Sure enough, they completed the task and had plenty of fodder for discussion, as they were free of the fear that all their ideas had to be great.

Spending time to grow yourself into an idea machine will improve your ability to envision enhancements, process improvements, and other strokes of brilliance that will endear you to your colleagues and earn you a superhero cape.

There are two parts to this equation. First, hang out where the ideas are. Second, train your brain to become an idea machine.

Hang Out Where the Ideas Are

Make it a practice to read blogs, browse system documentation and release notes, and peruse the Trailhead Community forums. Subscribe to the Salesforce Admin podcast and follow relevant hashtags on LinkedIn and Twitter. Ideas will jump off the page at you, and you'll find solutions to problems you never realized could be quickly addressed. We don't know what we don't know. Or what we've never had to investigate. Or functionality we haven't had time to explore. Go to the places where the collective community has a tremendous amount of knowledge and get ideas for all sorts of issues you can proactively address.

Believe it or not, some of my best sources of inspiration have been the help docs on the Salesforce Developers site describing formula operators and functions[6] and the help documentation that provides examples of advanced formula fields.[7] I know, nerd alert. But seriously, from win rates, distance calculations, and numerous ways to use hyperlinks to make magic happen with custom images, the examples provided have generated more ideas than I can count. This past year I decided to stop watching the news and logging into Facebook. Instead, I'm using that time to scroll through my LinkedIn feed and network with other Salesforce professionals, and I've been amazed by how much I've learned and how many great ideas I've seen there that I can shamelessly borrow.

A Real-Life Example

It's been well over a decade and I still recall the moment I was browsing the Salesforce Community site and stumbled on the very solution I needed to solve a major usability challenge. Multiple custom objects in my org had custom lookup fields that referenced the user object. For example, the Client Onboarding record included a lookup to the user assigned as the

Orientation Specialist. I needed to create dynamic list views and reports for the Orientation team that would return only records in which they were the assigned resource, similar to how you can use the out-of-the-box filter by owner criteria to show "My Records."

At the time, I didn't know how to do that for users who weren't the record owner. Instead, I trained users to create list views and reports by having each of them enter their name as the filter criteria. Yikes! This solution wasn't realistic, as most users weren't likely going to bother, and it meant we didn't have a curated set of reports that we could update as we added new fields or made other changes. However, I hadn't been actively looking for an answer to this challenge because it simply hadn't occurred to me that there was an easy fix.

One morning as I was browsing the Salesforce Community site, there it was! Someone had posed a question that described my exact scenario. And, right below it, the answer I needed: a formula that would return true or false if the current user is the person in the referenced lookup field.

Using this simple formula in a field I labeled "Orientation Specialist is Me" that didn't need to be visible on the page layout, I could filter reports and dashboards to dynamically show the records where the formula returned a value of true. All assigned team members could now report on their assignments using a standard report or list view! Not only did this discovery save me time and earn me tremendous kudos from my users for that use case, but over the years I've gotten tremendous mileage out of it.

Here's the formula if your org would benefit:

IF(Custom_Lookup_Field__c = $User.Id, 1,0)

Train Your Brain to Be an Idea Machine

So, the first step is to hang out where the ideas are. The second is to develop your brain into an idea machine. Like any other muscle, you can train your brain to cultivate ideas and train your inner critic to take a seat and let the creative juices flow. Altucher recommends a daily idea brainstorming session but cautions you not to stop after three ideas. That's easy. It's first getting past five and then to ten that will push your creativity and force you to dig deep into the realm of what's possible. You don't have to execute any or all of your ideas or even share them with anyone. Regular practice will build your idea muscle, and you'll inevitably stumble on a few that you can't stop thinking about that will grow into something of value. Most of these ideas will be throw-away, but you'll have some great ones in the bunch. The mere practice of establishing this habit will improve your ability to think creatively and dream up ideas without being limited by perfectionism.

I've included a list of topics you could start with for your first 10 days of idea generation. Don't stop there. Have a brainstorming session to come up with additional ideas. Commit to doing this daily for a month and see how you become more comfortable and adept at brainstorming solutions and creatively identifying problems that your Salesforce superpowers can solve.

TEN TOPICS FOR IDEA BRAINSTORMING SESSIONS

- Ten ways to collect user feedback

- Ten tips and tricks that would add value for your users

- Ten housekeeping projects needed in your org

- Ten things you could do with a macro in Service Cloud to streamline steps

- Ten ways to automate tasks you do to onboard or terminate users

- Ten things you might be able to get from your Salesforce account executive if you weren't afraid to ask

- Ten ways you could improve your org if you had unlimited resources

- Ten ways to enhance usability for a specific business unit or functional team

- Ten ways flow or quick actions could save clicks for your users

- Ten reports your stakeholders should have but probably don't

Can you see how building your idea muscle can yield all sorts of inspiration that will solve problems and provide insight into challenges you hadn't even thought to solve? Remember, the goal isn't to act on all these but to train your brain to be creative with the solutions you consider and go deep in thinking about different areas you can influence. See which ones germinate into that lightbulb idea. Run a few of these ideas by your stakeholders, as you may stumble onto the next thing that might be a game changer.

DOS AND DON'TS AS A VALUE-ADDING PROBLEM SOLVER

- **Do** listen to complaints, understand pain points, and pay attention to themes coming into your ticket queue to uncover hidden problems.

- **Do** make sure the problem you're solving is impacting more than one person. Admittedly, fixing a major issue for a key stakeholder and getting a few superhero points may be worth it, but you generally want to solve the most impactful organizational challenges.

- **Do** validate your assumptions.

- **Don't** just solve the immediate problem. Address the root cause, as this is not only a value add for your stakeholders, but it will result in fewer tickets in your queue.

CHAPTER 9:

BE PROACTIVE

Whatever the problem, be part of the solution. Don't just sit around raising questions and pointing out obstacles.

—Tina Fey

Each of the Salesforce admin pro behaviors we've discussed requires you to be inherently proactive in probing the issues, suggesting process improvements, and getting to the root causes of problems. Being proactive is part and parcel of everything you do, but some specific preemptive actions are worth calling out. This chapter covers three ways to apply your Salesforce awesomeness in a forward-looking manner. I'm including the concept referred to earlier of adding bonus features, the extras you configure above and beyond any implicit requirements to improve usability or provide a more comprehensive solution. I'll also discuss steps you can take to prevent problems from occurring and, when issues do surface, ensure that you find them before your users do.

Add Things They Would Never Think to Ask For

In Louisiana, the Cajuns use the term Lagniappe, which roughly translates to giving folks a little something unexpected or extra, like a 13th donut with the purchase of a dozen. In the Salesforce space, a little something extra equates to all those useful items you include above and beyond what was requested. These are the collection of little things that users will love and remember. In the product management world, they're often referred to as "delighters," as they yield a disproportionate increase in customer joy. Whatever we call them, they are the elements our stakeholders wouldn't think to ask for or wouldn't imagine would be easy to implement that improve usability and provide a more comprehensive end-to-end solution.

Several years ago, my team completed an incredibly complex approval process with more than 100 permutations in the approval matrix. Despite all the manual steps we eliminated, the element that generated the most positive user feedback were the images we displayed using a formula field that showed silly graphics as a visual indicator of the approval status. The users loved that and started asking for something similar on all their key page layouts.

Go where the ideas are and see what other Salesforce admins are doing that might add value for your users. Rev up your creativity to consider where you can utilize your Salesforce admin craftiness to give them a little something extra that packs a punch.

Salesforce lets you shine in this regard by providing many different ways to generate quick wins to multiply your value points with relatively low effort. For example, if your users make high-volume calls and manually track all their activity, give them an "easy button" that will log a completed task with "Left message" in the subject field and, at the same time, schedule a follow-up task one day later. If your Inside Sales team prioritizes activities based on time zone, add a formula field to display this, maybe with the bonus of showing the weather in that location to give them a conversation starter. If your users regularly access data from another system, create a dynamic link that passes through specific details from the Salesforce record so they can navigate to the information they need with one click. Users love and remember these little conveniences.

Remember that example we discussed a few chapters back that resulted in a custom object for Gwen, who was initiating a new certification program for her franchisees? Based on that scenario, what bonus features might you have included in your demo when you walked Gwen through the proposed solution? What small things would be easy to implement to add value for her team? Adding these things is where it gets fun, as everyone brings their creativity to bear a little differently. Here are a few examples:

- Add an image field on the Certification object with a visual indicator, such as a red or green flag, to display the Status field's value.

- Activate Salesforce Path using values from the Status field and celebrate with virtual confetti when the process is complete.

- Use a custom graphic for the Certification object's custom tab icon. Suppose you asked if there was Marketing support for the program and uncovered a logo explicitly created for the certification program. Why not incorporate that?

These items are win-wins from a Salesforce admin perspective, as they're relatively easy to configure yet earn massive points. Over time, you'll likely have a host of signature add-ons you regularly include in any deployment where they make sense. The possibilities will continue to grow as your Salesforce admin toolkit expands with Lightning components and other new and improved ways to wow.

Examples of Bonus Features

- Add dynamic report links or report charts to the page layout

- Use emojis as visual indicators in list views, in formula fields on page layouts, and even as default field values

- Add freebie components or apps from AppExchange

- Enable the account logo setting

- Enable autocomplete on standard addresses

- Enable Social Accounts to provide easy access to social network profiles

- Add conditional highlighting to reports and dashboards
- Use roll-up summary fields to highlight or summarize critical dates or amounts

 ## CAUTION! A CALM-THE-CHAOS CAVEAT

In the spirit of guarding your time—a precious commodity for the Salesforce admin—when adding these bonus features, make sure they're legitimate quick hits in terms of the amount of time it takes to configure them. It makes sense to allocate a little extra time to make additions if they are easy to implement, high value, and unlikely to result in throw-away work. When you have ideas about implementing new features or automation that would take more time to design and configure, validate the proposed approach with your stakeholder before spending time with your hands on the keyboard.

Use Checklists Before Go Live

Specific configuration details such as search and mini page layouts are seldom included in a requirements document because they aren't things business users notice or think about in advance. When done right, these are just an intuitive part of their Salesforce user experience, but done wrong, Ouch! You will overwhelm your business partners with choices if you walk in with a clipboard and ask, "What fields do you want on your search layout? What fields do you want on your tab layout? In what order should we display each related list?" They'll probably have no idea what you mean.

Instead, add value by making your best guess based on what you know about their business process. Then, as you walk through the functionality, point out the configurable items and encourage feedback if any adjustments are needed.

Be proactive to ensure that these details are accounted for, as they are the small things that will make or break the user experience. Similarly, little stuff like inconsistency in punctuation and field names or spelling errors can make a difference in how users perceive the system's quality, so include these on your list of things to double-check.

NITTY-GRITTY DETAIL CHECKLIST

✓ Items that are not needed, such as buttons, tabs, and related lists, are removed from the page layout

✓ Search layouts are configured

✓ All page layouts have a mini page layout set up

✓ Default list views are configured

✓ All list views are neat and tidy and exposed only to the groups that need to see them

✓ Related lists display the appropriate fields in the correct order without unnecessary buttons

✓ Punctuation and capitalization are correct and consistent on all field labels

✓ No two fields have the same label name

✓ Field labels are as self-explanatory as possible

✓ Field-level help text is populated where applicable and contains correct grammar, punctuation, and spelling

✓ Grammar, punctuation, and spelling are correct on all dashboard titles, subtitles, and footers

Pro tip: Reviewing field-level help text and field labels may not be your best use of time, especially because some of us don't have an eye for grammatical details. Since this doesn't require Salesforce skills, it's a perfect task to hand off. I promise there are people with eagle eyes on your team who can't sleep at night knowing there may be typos and inconsistencies. Ask your boss to help identify a proofreader or recruit volunteers as needed.

Plan for What Could Go Wrong and Have a Proactive Plan to Monitor

As the saying goes, we should hope for the best but prepare for the worst. Proactive Salesforce admins anticipate problems and build the mechanisms to identify them as soon as they arise. If something goes wrong with the solution you deploy or if it isn't being used as expected, strive to be the first to notice. You are a preemptive problem solver when you call your business partner to let them know you see something wonky. When they have to contact you because they see something wonky, they start to wonder if it was right in the first place. The more production issues they find, the more doubt they have about the system and, frankly, your ability to keep watch. So any new functionality or automation you deploy should include mechanisms to proactively monitor to ensure that all is working as expected, especially if it's business critical.

Don't wait for the call. Brainstorm what could go wrong and spend some time thinking about exception reports that would provide visibility if any of those things happen. Having reports or dashboards to monitor system automation and identify data integrity issues increases the likelihood of addressing issues before they become problems. Your monitoring dashboards will have a different focus than the business-facing dashboards used by your functional leaders and business teams.

Suppose you've implemented automation to facilitate the process by which your Services team initiates client onboarding activities. A record, specifically a custom object called Solution Delivery, gets created every time Team Sales closes a deal. Your monitoring dashboard might include metrics to identify closed Opportunities without an associated Solution Delivery record or Opportunity records that erroneously have more than one related record. If you included logic in your automation, such as assigning a Solution Delivery record type or routing to a delivery team based on the Opportunity product family, you might include components to validate that the logic is firing as expected.

While those reports will tell you whether the automation is working as expected, with your product management hat on, you'll want to create additional reporting to gauge how the users interact with the new functionality and assess whether it is meeting the business objectives.

Your dashboard might have some "How are they using it?" widgets that group records by key fields so you can see what data they are entering, or it may have a metric that shows the number of records in which a critical but not required field is blank. If a stated objective was to shrink the days between a deal closing and the client-kick-off meeting, you might track how this number is trending. In addition to letting you be the first to spot any technical issues, monitoring dashboards allow you to proactively spot things that can be tweaked or iterated within the application or business process, reinforcing your value add.

A Picture for Perspective

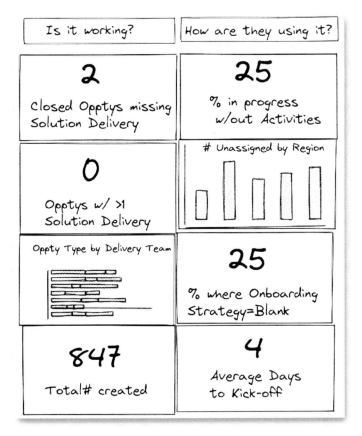

This monitoring dashboard includes widgets to ensure that the automation is working as expected and the new functionality is being adopted and meeting the business objectives.

Pro tip: Work hard to find bugs. If you have a formal QA team, take them to lunch as frequently as possible because they're your unsung heroes. Don't take it personally if they use words like "bugs" and document "defects" to identify things you need to fix. That's standard language in the software world and not a knock on your work. Finding those before you move your changes to production enables you to deliver quality solutions, so celebrate every issue they uncover. If you don't have a QA team, make sure you're testing your work and have at least a second set of eyes on all changes before they go into production. Depending on the type and scope of changes, you may need to log in as various users to test whether the functionality works correctly across all user groups and profiles.

Pro tip: Make it a practice at least once a quarter to log in as a user in each active profile and cruise around their page layouts to ensure everything is in order. Despite our best intentions, the process for deploying changes and installing AppExchange apps makes it easy to inadvertently drop something onto a page or display an unnecessary tab. Plus, it will allow you to see if anything has become outdated due to business changes, then proactively suggest it as a system enhancement.

CHAPTER 10:

COMMUNICATE LIKE A SALESFORCE PRO

Don't follow the crowd, let the crowd follow you.

—Margaret Thatcher

Communication is an inherent part of the activities and practices that earn you the Salesforce pro moniker. Active listening, asking probing questions, and providing context are all critical communication skills. How you communicate directly impacts your status and authority. When done right, your words and approach to communicating with your stakeholders can significantly contribute to your building a fan base and reinforce your expertise. Conversely, a few things can erode your hard-earned goodwill and ability to influence, both of which are essential to getting out of order-taker mode.

Here are five ways to ensure that what you say and how you say it puts points on the board and doesn't detract from your efforts.

Articulate Your Point of View (POV)

Your constituents aren't experts in Salesforce. You are! You know the system, the data, and the platform's capabilities. You are not there to simply absorb information and then execute whatever people want. Your value is inherently tied to the ideas you bring to the table. People need your guidance, your advice. You have a point of view that can and should inform and influence decisions. Your point of view is an essential element of your expertise. You've seen this in action across the scenarios detailed so far. Digging in to uncover business needs and proposing the right solution even when it's slightly different from what they asked for is a perfect example. Be confident in what you know and the value of your Salesforce experience.

Take time to consider your POV before presenting information. When there are options to discuss, decide in advance what you think the right course of action is and be prepared to say why. Don't wait for people to ask what you think. Instead, frame the conversation and then drive toward mutual benefit. Your point of view won't always win, but sharing your perspective is essential in getting your constituents to realize the value your opinions and influence provide.

An added benefit of articulating your POV is that it can speed up meetings and decision-making. You can move the ball forward and display leadership by proposing solutions. Leverage your POV and put a proposal on the table. People can respond faster and more thoroughly with a proposition to consider instead of a blank page.

Sharing your POV can be difficult when you're just starting your career. It can be challenging to speak up when you're new in your role or have a less-senior title. Expressing your perspective can be especially challenging when your point of view may be different than other people's. Trust me; I've been there many times. Recognize the value you bring by sharing your expertise and perspective. The more you express your POV and propose a direction forward, the more comfortable you'll get. Start paying attention to opportunities to flex this muscle and practice doing it whenever you can.

TALK TRACKS:

Articulating your POV

Instead of What do you think?
Try I suggest…How does that sound?

Instead of Here are the five topics we need to discuss. Where do you want to start?
Try Here are the topics we need to discuss based on the order of importance. Is there anything else you want to cover? Do you agree with this prioritization?

Instead of Which project workstreams should we tackle first?
Try In reviewing all the workstreams, I believe these two are the logical starting place because they impact the most people. Does anyone feel differently?

Instead of How do you think we should group the stories for the upcoming releases?
Try I recommend deploying the five stories relating to the Lead record and grouping the Opportunity record changes in the following release. Do you agree with this approach?

Pro tip: Practice presenting your POV on noncontroversial topics. When your team can't decide where to order lunch, propose a restaurant. When your colleagues are wishy-washy about the frequency of meetings for a particular topic, suggest the right cadence.

Be Clear about Whether You're Expressing an Opinion or a Firm Conviction

This is good advice in all facets of life, but it's particularly relevant to the Salesforce admin. There is a difference between when you simply *have an opinion* and when you *feel strongly* about something. If you feel strongly about a design decision, process recommendation, or suggested course of action, voice it accordingly. As you articulate your perspective, being clear on how strongly you feel about it is part of the message.

 TALK TRACKS:

Clarifying Opinion vs. Firm Conviction

➢ Clarifying that **it is an opinion:** I would go with the second option, but I don't feel strongly either way.

➢ Clarifying that **it is a firm conviction:** I feel strongly about this. I am happy to discuss my reasoning in detail, but under no circumstances can I recommend that approach.

Think Like a Lobbyist

Like a lobbyist, you will sometimes need to be strategic and work some "behind-the-scenes magic" to influence stakeholders or get them to consider a different point of view. When there is dissension in the ranks or a complicated issue about which there will likely be strong opinions and different perspectives, discuss the matter with key participants before raising it in a larger group setting. If you're proposing something, do you have buy-in? Do they agree? If not, get to the heart of their concerns so you have time to address or alleviate them before calling the proverbial vote. Having this conversation in advance also provides your audience time to digest the information.

When the group convenes, you should know all parties' opinions and facilitate the dialogue accordingly. Group dynamics are different than those of personal interactions. Group discussions should never be the forum for initiating controversial ideas or sharing bad news for the first time. Control the message.

Err on the side of Overcommunication

Surprises are great for kids but not stakeholders. As a rule of thumb, you want to err on the side of overcommunication to ensure that your business partners are aligned with what you are and are not working on for them, and where things stand with each initiative. In my experience, most things that cause heartburn on Salesforce projects rarely have anything to do with system bugs. If there's something awry, whether it's an unhappy business stakeholder or an unhappy you, a misunderstanding or communication gap often is at the heart of the matter. Perhaps something needs to be clarified or the elephant in the room needs discussion.

When it feels like things aren't quite jiving, when you're hearing your stakeholder reference dates, deadlines, or deliverables different from what you've agreed to, or if it's been a while since you connected other than through email, pick up the phone and have a conversation. I learned this during my years in sales. We used to say that if you hadn't talked to your prospect lately, your deal was probably dead; you just didn't know it yet. If it's been a while since you've had a live connection with a key stakeholder, particularly if you have a significant initiative in flight, there may be issues swirling under the surface. Reach out to check in, ensure that you are on the same page, and ferret out any hot topics.

As a good rule of thumb, certain situations warrant direct communication (not email):

- When you're slammed and haven't had a chance to start on their request

- When there's a project delay

- When something is not working as expected

No one wants bad news by email. Even if you ultimately need to send an email to document a decision, no interested parties should be hearing negative or surprising information through this channel. Pick up the phone. To the extent possible, include a proposed solution or a few options to remedy the situation, understanding that this is not always possible if time is of the essence. In that case, note that you are working on alternative approaches and will respond as quickly as possible with options. We are all human and things happen. Your business stakeholders are likely to understand when you communicate with honesty and immediacy and bring a solution to the problem.

Sorry/Not Sorry

Speaking of being human, own it when you screw up. If you lost your temper, said something rude, dropped the ball, or overslept and missed the meeting, you should apologize.

However, you are not personally responsible for all the things that can and do go wrong in your Salesforce system, with the technology you're using, or with all the moving parts that must come together to deploy a Salesforce solution. You don't need to apologize for things that have nothing to do with you. When you do, it diminishes your authority and minimizes all the valuable work you do contribute.

If the project is late because you couldn't stop binge-watching *Game of Thrones*, you owe the team an apology. But I'm willing to bet that if your project is behind schedule or the demo didn't go quite as planned, there were probably multiple reasons that had nothing to do with you.

Maybe someone didn't get you the data in time. Maybe the Internet connection in your office was slow, causing pages to time out. Perhaps that pesky formula compilation error popped up, necessitating much more time and complexity to populate a simple date field. Or maybe you had to jump on a production issue right before the deadline.

When things out of your control happen, acknowledge them, but don't hang your head and give away your power. If you are the one who saved the day, if anything, you should get credit. In these situations, simply thank your constituents for their patience. This can be difficult if you typically accept accountability for getting things done and anything that goes haywire. But pay attention to whether you are throwing out an inappropriate apology and see the difference it makes to eliminate that word.

 TALK TRACKS:

Eliminating Unnecessary Apologies

Instead of I'm sorry it took so long to get you this document.

Try Thank you for your patience while we worked to prepare the document.

Instead of Apologies that this demo is later than we originally agreed.

Try We appreciated your patience while we worked through the preparation required to show this functionality today.

Instead of Sorry this meeting got rescheduled five times.

Try Thank you for your flexibility and patience while we coordinated schedules to find a meeting time that worked for everyone.

While we are on the subject of not apologizing for things that aren't your fault, I can't leave this topic without mentioning something we previously discussed regarding the importance of voicing your opinion. Do not apologize simply because you have a different view. You are an expert in your field, and part of your job is to ensure that you communicate your ideas, even if they don't always jive with others'. Just say it. Take the emotion out of it. It is your responsibility to put your opinion on the table. Similarly, I often hear colleagues apologizing because they have a question. If you need more information, ask. There is no reason to apologize unless you were late to the meeting or multitasking and, therefore, missed something already said.

State your differing opinion, be polite and professional, and get the information you need without apologizing. Start paying attention to the apologies you hear or say in the work setting and you'll see that they can diminish a statement before it's even made.

 ## TALK TRACKS:

More Sorry/Not Sorry

Instead of Sorry, but I have to disagree. I think it would make more sense if the process worked the other way because…

Try Great point, but I see it a little differently than you do. I think it would make more sense if the process worked the other way because.·..

Instead of Sorry, but I have a question.

Try I appreciate the information you shared and need some clarity.

PART 1 WRAP-UP

Great job getting through the first part of this book! I hope you picked up a few ideas to try.

First you've got to come to the table with an ownership mindset and core knowledge about your company, your users, and your org. You add value and create a cadre of raving fans by uncovering needs, proactively solving problems, and meeting business requirements with the best Salesforce solution.

Here are the six Salesforce admin pro competencies we covered with a little bold text and a rhyme to help you remember them.

SIX WAYS TO SHOW YOU'RE A SALESFORCE PRO

- **Pro**be to find out what they really need

- **Pro**vide expert advice

- **Pro**duce data insights and actionable ideas

- Take a page from **pro**duct management

- Solve **pro**blems, even ones they don't know they have

- Be **pro**active

Can you see how applying these concepts can elevate how stakeholders view your role? Do you notice how the skills build on each other, allowing you to exponentially add value as you layer on what you've learned? As you make a conscious effort to start incorporating these, you'll begin to stack up wins and see the differences in your relationships with your constituents.

Now hold on to your many Salesforce admin hats, as we're not finished yet. We established the Salesforce admin conundrum early on: the more value you deliver, the faster and more furiously the demands and competing projects seem to come. In the next part of the book, you'll learn how to establish processes, practice techniques, and set business boundaries to guard against overwhelm and keep the chaos at bay.

PART 2:

CALM THE CHAOS

CHAPTER 11:

PROCESSES TO PROVIDE A METHOD TO THE MADNESS

Though this be madness, yet there is method in't.

—William Shakespeare

Here's a guiding principle: Process and procedures provide protection. I'm going a little overboard on the Salesforce pro wordplay, but I hope it will help you remember the importance of this. Establishing processes regarding how you intake, track, and prioritize work protects you from being the villain. It gives you cover. Having defined processes for how you deliver Salesforce solutions will set expectations with your stakeholders and train your constituents to work with you more sustainably.

There's an added benefit. Your stakeholders will appreciate having processes, even if they are sometimes resistant at first. People want to know what to expect. They like transparency. They want to know how their work will be prioritized, when you will complete it, what things they are responsible for, and what ongoing support you will provide.

This chapter introduces seven processes you can incorporate to bring order to your work, allowing you to continue ratcheting up your points while seeing a corresponding drop in chaos.

Track All Requests Using a Ticketing System

Whether you refer to them as tickets or user stories, all requests for Salesforce support should be documented and managed through a ticketing system. Full stop. This means you do not make changes requested through your in-box, IM feed, or "Hey, can you please add a field?" Slack message.

The headline here is twofold. First, you must have a ticketing system. Second, you must train your peeps that you cannot work on changes, enhancements, or troubleshooting without a corresponding ticket. If you already have a tracking mechanism, be it something built on the Salesforce platform, Jira, ServiceNow, or something else, feel free to skip to the second part of this section, where we look at how to ensure that opening a ticket is the only mechanism for intake.

If you don't already use a ticketing system, read this section and get started on your action plan to get one. Seriously. It's that important.

Here are six reasons having a ticketing system is critical:

- **It provides measurable data points** about your volume of work. These metrics can help you make a case for additional resources.

- **It provides an audit trail** of what changes were requested and a place for you to load artifacts such as success and error files following a data load.

- **It saves you from spending too much time** going back and forth, as you can train users to include all the information you need, even screenshots.

- **It provides a place to document the rationale** for a solution and considerations related to the solutioning process. Capturing this information will save you and future Salesforce admins tons of time you might otherwise have spent trying to troubleshoot or understand how and why something was implemented.

- **It gives you one place** to track all outstanding requests with structured data such as type, date submitted, and status. This approach is critical in staying organized, establishing an appropriate follow-up cadence, and prioritizing work.

- **It provides an orderly method for collaborating** with people for review, approval, or re-assignment if they are better suited to address the issue.

Like most things in the Salesforce world, there are many ways to implement a ticketing system. Depending on your role in the organization, you may or may not have a say in this process. If it is something you can influence, the path of least resistance is building your ticket queue in Salesforce. Not only is it where your users are already working, but you also get the added benefit of a real-world canvas where you can try out new Salesforce features and functionality.

Your ticketing system doesn't need to be complicated. You'll want a status field and a picklist to categorize requests to differentiate ticket types such as bugs, administrator requests, data loads, and feature enhancements. Other than that, you can start with something as simple as giving your users a big text field so they can tell you what they need.

A Picture for Perspective

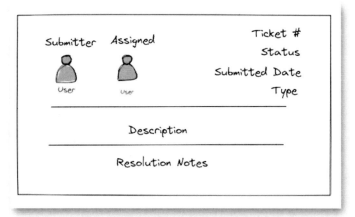

Even the most basic ticket tracking system will have tremendous benefits regarding your ability to organize and prioritize your work.

While you can keep it simple, a ticketing system on the Salesforce platform provides a great low-risk way to experiment with new features and try functionality that otherwise might not have a use case in your organization.

For example, I once worked with a team that used a custom object called SOS, an acronym for Sales Ops Support, for their tickets. When Salesforce announced they were retiring the Notes & Attachments object, we implemented the Notes and Files objects as part of the SOS process to learn the nuances of both before deploying them in other parts of the org. We also worked on our SOS tickets using Lightning when it first came out to get comfortable with the interface before transitioning any users.

Want to try your hand with approvals? Is there new flow functionality you haven't had a chance to use? What about the numerous enhancements that keep making Lightning pages more dynamic? You might consider linking tickets to other custom objects to group your work by project or workstreams. Put your Salesforce consulting hat on and explore how you can improve the user experience or automate work for the admin team, and you'll give yourself some hands-on-keyboard expertise in the process.

 Pro tip: Consider where it makes sense to include dynamic links that open a ticket from within Salesforce to make it easy for your users to get help. For instance, if your process is such that your users request assistance when they need duplicate company records merged, include a dynamic link or button on the Account page that passes through the record ID of the Account and the running user and then prepopulates the ticket type value "Merge Account" to save some keystrokes.

Think Twice Before Leveraging Service Cloud for Ticketing

It's tempting to leverage Service Cloud functionality for a ticketing system. After all, Service Cloud does that for a living and does a mighty fine job. Nevertheless, I encourage you not to go down that road. Instead, for two reasons, use a custom object.

First, you may eventually want to extend the use of the Salesforce platform, and therefore your ticketing system, to users who don't require a Sales Cloud or Service Cloud license. You would hate for your ticketing system to be the reason to incur a more expensive charge for users who otherwise don't need access to the Case object. (Hint: As of this writing, several platform license types provide cost-effective options to license users who only require access to custom objects and not the core CRM features.)

Second, even if your company is not using Service Cloud functionality, you may eventually want to leverage Service Cloud for a customer-facing use case. Of course, the platform can support different processes through functionality such as record types and assignment rules. Still, unless Service Cloud was specifically purchased for managing internal employee support, it's usually more trouble than it's worth. Please trust me; you'll be glad you can easily separate your Salesforce admin ticketing system from your company's external support process.

Tickets Are the Only Method for Intake: No Exceptions

Once you have a ticket system in place, the equally important part of the equation is ensuring that all requests come to you through the ticket queue. When a user sends you a request in an email, let them know it needs to go through your ticketing system. The first time this happens, you can enter the ticket and send them a link to let them know you took care of it. If they continue going around the ticketing system, you have to be stern, but you can always blame "the policy," which may or may not be an actual thing, and say you'd love to help but aren't permitted to work on any request that doesn't come through the queue.

Suppose you are partnering with stakeholders on new functionality, enhancement ideas, new dashboards, or similar initiatives. In that case, you might be the one to enter the ticket to track the work. Regardless of who writes it up, having structured tracking for all requested changes and outstanding to-dos keeps you organized and is critical to managing your backlog, which we'll discuss in an upcoming section.

TALK TRACKS:

Directing Users to Create Tickets

➢ As a policy reminder, we can't change the system or data without a corresponding ticket. I've added this one for you: [hyperlink]. In the future, please send these through as tickets to ensure that I can assist.

➢ Please log a ticket instead of sending me an email when you have issues like this. Multiple people manage our queue so we can triage critical items. This way, if I'm out unavailable, someone else will be able to assist you.

Pro tip: Give status updates often. People are patient as long as they know where they are in the queue. When you're underwater, you can generate an incredible amount of goodwill with a quick email or Chatter along the lines of "Haven't forgotten you. Had a few fire drills, but you're next."

A Real-Life Example: Tickets Provide Metrics to Make a Case for More Resources

A ticketing system provides the evidence to make a compelling business case for additional resources or relief from tight timelines by illustrating the volume, pace, and severity of all the items coming your way.

I recently met a Salesforce admin seeking a new job who was the sole support for a Sales Cloud instance with 600 users. She shared that her frustration stemmed from being slammed and not having the resources to appropriately assist so many users, despite multiple conversations with her boss. I'm all for advocating for the correct resource allocation as a critical component of a calm-the-chaos strategy, so I asked her what metrics she used to make her case. Crickets. I asked how she tracked her support requests and system changes, and she said she took requests from IM, Outlook, and Chatter. No wonder her plea was falling on deaf ears. The absence of a structured intake process meant she could not articulate the volume of support tickets and enhancements she was managing and executing. Imagine how different her conversation might have gone had she been able to quantify that she had responded to 75 report requests, completed 125 data loads, resolved 300 user questions, and implemented 50 system enhancements during the year.

Show your Steps Salesforce Style

Show your work. Remember the instructions you received as a kid for doing math homework? Show the specific steps you go through to execute the problem. This gave your teacher insight into exactly how you tackled it and made it easy to identify a missed step or error. Plus, writing down each step provided documentation you could refer to if needed when solving a similar problem.

It's equally important when executing Salesforce work that you track your steps. Not only will solid documentation serve you and future admins well, it will save you time and minimize errors as you move solutions from a sandbox into production. As DevOps tools become more pervasive and admin-friendly, automated change tracking may one day make this recommendation unnecessary. Still, I'm willing to bet that in the meantime, this tip will add tremendous value to how you organize your work and collaborate with colleagues.

Years ago, I was fortunate to inherit an org that had been configured with a custom object for tracking system modifications (mods, as we called them). Over the years, I've replicated this functionality in all the orgs I've supported. It has saved me countless hours in terms of staying organized when delivering large enhancements or referencing past changes. Equally important, it has eliminated teamwide surprises, as we know exactly what metadata or code changes colleagues will be deploying. When introducing this concept to admins not accustomed to managing work in a structured format, I sometimes get that "You gotta be kidding" look. But after experiencing the benefits, they inevitably share they don't know how they ever worked without their trusty mods.

Memorialize with Mods

The Modification object is a simple way to track each change you make in Salesforce in a structured manner. Mods ensure that you have every click documented and can easily identify all the components to include in a change set or whatever deployment approach you use. If you manage your tickets and stories in Salesforce, this would be a child object with a one-to-many relationship to whatever object you use for that purpose. The ticket will contain the user story or request, so you'll know who requested it and why, and any notes needed to document the reason for a particular approach. The mods tell the story of exactly what steps you took to implement that solution.

Every unique element that needs to be included in a change set or deployment package and any steps that must be manually executed should have a corresponding mod. For instance, if you create a new field, add it to two different page layouts, and then do a data load to populate it, you would have four mods documented. At first it may seem like extra work, but you've got to track your changes somewhere, especially for more-complex enhancements.

You can track your mods with just a few key fields:

- **Action:** What are you doing? This can be captured in a picklist with the values Add, Modify, and Delete.

- **Where:** Essentially, on which object is the change taking place? If you take the recommendation in Chapter 2 and create an Object Overview object, this field can be a lookup relationship to that object. Alternatively, you can maintain a picklist of all the objects in your org. Some changes aren't object-specific, so you won't want to make this a required field.

- **What:** What exactly are you modifying? This is a picklist with everything you can change in the system, ranging from fields to flows to an Apex class. I recommend starting with the values on the Component Type picklist used when adding items to a Change Set.

- **Label:** The label name of the component you're changing.

- **API Name:** The API name of the component you're changing.

- **Comments:** A long text field for capturing notes about the modification.

It's that simple. Once the object is in place, as you're working in your sandbox in one window, use your second monitor to enter your mods and track your work. (Please tell me you're using two monitors. If not, stop reading and order a second one immediately. Even if you can't expense a second one, it will be worth every penny. Consider this an essential tool for comparing data and working in different environments—just don't use it as an excuse to multitask).

A Picture for Perspective

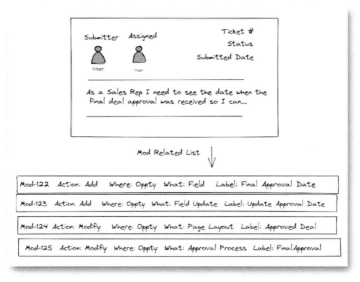

This ticket represents an enhancement request to auto-populate a new field on the Opportunity when the final step in a specific approval process is complete. The related list shows all the associated mods needed to complete the request.

```
Name       Mod-12345

Story #    SF-2344

Action:      Add

  What:      Field

 Where:      Opportunity

 Label:      Final Approval Date

   API:      Final_Approval_Date__c

        ┌──────────────────────────────────────────────────┐
        │              Field Details                       │
        │  (This section is visible only if What = Field)  │
        └──────────────────────────────────────────────────┘

                       Field can be visible/read-only to all profiles.
  FLS Details:

                       This field will auto-populate with the
  Help Text:           date when the final approval is received.

        ┌──────────────────────────────────────────────────┐
        │        Sandbox / Deployment Details              │
        └──────────────────────────────────────────────────┘

    In QA      ☑        Is Manual Step?    ☐

    In UAT     ☐        Deployment Notes:

    In Prod    ☐
```

This Mod tracks the addition of the "Final Approval Date" field on the Opportunity. The Mod page layout includes a dynamic section to capture requirements for field-level security (FLS) and help text that is only visible when the "What" indicates a change to a field.

The teams I've worked with have found tremendous benefit in leveraging the Modification object in various creative ways. Here are some examples illustrating how mods can improve Salesforce admin efficiency and productivity.

- **Use checkboxes** to confirm that each item referenced in the mod has been added to a change set or deployment package. To ensure that you include all the pieces and parts, compare the number of mods to the number of change set components. You can add fields for each sandbox required for your development process so that the mod can document that changes have made their way through the correct environments.

- **Add workflow or reports** to ensure that the Dev team reviews certain changes, such as adding or modifying validation rules—which require extra checking to prevent disruption to existing integrations or test classes—before deployment.

- **Export a mod report** to facilitate business approvals or assist the team working on the release notes.

- **Leverage mods** to provide direction for team members who execute deployments on your behalf, as mods serve as a checklist for all required components and manual steps. Provide dynamic report links on your story/ticket object to make it easy to see and organize related records.

Review Your Queue with a Different View

"Reviewing your queue with a different view" means regularly scheduling time to view all open requests and issues through a slightly different lens, depending on what you're trying to accomplish. Your queue likely contains a mix of "administrivia," including quick-hit admin tasks, troubleshooting requests, end-user questions, and more-complex enhancement requests, or "stories" in the Agile world. You probably have plenty of new and in-flight tickets, coupled with others hanging around untouched either because they're nice-to-haves or you keep running out of time.

It's important to have regularity and rigor in reviewing your queue to identify and move forward anything that has been long forgotten, remove anything irrelevant, and flag what's suddenly important if business priorities have changed. Regular queue reviews ensure that you're working on the right things as determined by both business priorities and the need to keep the lights on for the teams and individuals using the system.

During the backlog review (defined below), you will review a set of stories with your stakeholders to understand and prioritize the requested body of work. At other times during the week, day, or month, you'll want to review your open tickets to ensure that you understand the urgency and can triage accordingly, particularly if you are responsible for time-sensitive tasks, such as user administration and troubleshooting.

Formalize a Backlog Review with Your Stakeholders

Your backlog refers to the list of open tasks and enhancement requests in your queue. It should be a prioritized list of items you've agreed to work on, plus all the other stuff further down the to-do list, including the random requests you haven't yet committed to but don't want to forget or keep in your inbox. During the backlog review, often called a refinement or grooming session in the Agile world, you review your tickets with stakeholders for relevance and priority. You discuss any required sequencing for business reasons, training considerations, or technical dependencies. You partner with your stakeholders to determine the right next work based on their business objectives and your knowledge of what's involved with executing the request. Yep, there's that product management hat again!

Depending on your areas of responsibility, you may have separate sessions with different stakeholders. For instance, you may hold individual monthly meetings with both your Service Cloud and Sales Cloud business owners to review their enhancement requests, bug fixes, and relevant season release updates. The meeting objective is to ensure that you understand their desired outcomes and priorities and align on the work you'll do and the general order in which you'll do it. This includes specifying work you *won't* be doing to eliminate any expectation that you're working on something not on your docket.

Your backlog review should consist of the following:

- Removing or deprioritizing stories that are no longer relevant

- Reviewing new issues and enhancement requests

- Prioritizing items as nice-to-have and must-have

- Reviewing significant pieces of work to determine how to decompose into smaller chunks and deploy an iterative MVP approach

- Identifying dependencies, including items that require a significant amount of time or information from your stakeholder

Where does this activity fit in your calm-the-chaos strategy? You risk wasting effort without a shared understanding of what you will work on and in which order. You could complete items that aren't important while missing the essential ones. There's an opportunity cost for every story you work on, so you and your business partners must align on what will get done and what will have to wait.

All stories are not created equal. Make sure your business partners understand that you'll be sequencing work based on priority and complexity. Sometimes stories that aren't the most important are simple to execute. You may be able to knock some easy things out here and there, whereas you may require a focused block of time to complete more-complex requirements.

Do you have a junior admin or trainee to do rote system tasks? You can likely assign some tickets to this person, which means some simple stories will probably be completed before others that your business partner may have indicated are high priority.

Your stakeholders also need to recognize that some work isn't optional. You may have technical debt, system optimization, or required changes to support a seasonal release. These things may need to get done to keep the system functioning, regardless of business priorities. Regular communication and transparency around what you're working on *and why* will go a long way toward maintaining great stakeholder relationships.

Pro tip: Just because you define something as a production bug doesn't mean it needs to be first on your priority list. Suppose you have an issue that only happens in a rare edge case, particularly if it's something you can proactively identify with a report or an email alert. Investing time and energy in addressing that bug may not be the best bang for your buck. Similarly, if you find a bug that has been there for months, it may be harmless enough that it can wait a few more weeks while you work on higher-value items. Use your backlog review session to ensure that you and your business partners agree on where bug fixes fall on the priority list.

Keep Your House in Order

The backlog review with your stakeholders isn't a replacement for regularly reviewing your queue on your own, with different vantage points at key intervals throughout the day or week. Here are other ways to assess your queue:

Review as a first responder. In the morning and a few times each day, do a quick check to identify anything that requires immediate attention. You're looking for production issues and legitimately urgent requests for system access, data loads, etc. Is anything preventing users from doing their work? Is there any request that truly can't wait? If you share this responsibility with other admins on your team, I recommend taking shifts to read and triage tickets to ensure that you aren't duplicating efforts by having each team member read every incoming ticket.

During an urgency review, the goal is to identify immediate issues, not go into the weeds with nice-to-haves or tasks you can execute during the time you set aside for standard queue work. If Mary from Marketing has submitted a request for new fields she wants for an upcoming campaign, there's no reason to read this request in detail when reviewing for urgency. However, it may be worth taking the time to categorize it so you don't have to touch it twice. Only do that if you can assess it without going too deep into the rabbit hole. Now is not the time to ponder whether Team Marketing is using even half of the fields they requested on the campaign object. That's important but not relevant during a time slot for triage.

Review as a traffic cop. At least once a week, depending on the volume of incoming tickets, review the queue as if you were directing traffic. Look for aged tickets, high-impact tickets that appear to be stuck, and any still open because you're waiting for information. Take action if needed. Send a second request if someone's holding you up. Pick up the phone and get details if a question in the ticket isn't clear. During this pass, you'll also want to ensure that dates, status values, and other parameters are accurate and up to date.

Review with truth serum. At times you may need to keep yourself honest. Is there something you've been avoiding in your queue like a letter from the IRS? In my experience, this is usually due to one of two reasons: you don't understand the request or issue or you don't know how to resolve it. If it's the first, pick up the phone and clarify. Ask if they can share their screen or provide screenshots to show you what they mean. Rest assured that if it's the second, you don't always have to know the answer. You can and should "phone a friend," be that reaching out to your boss or another admin on your team or leveraging the Salesforce community when you're unclear how to execute something or can't get to the bottom of an issue. Make sure you've done your due diligence and can clearly articulate the problem, and share any theories you may have or steps you've taken to investigate before you take up someone's time.

Review as a Salesforce business analyst. Are you using your Salesforce admin magic to make *yourself* more effective? Your expertise includes assessing processes to determine how to improve efficiency through technology or by rethinking the approach. At least once a quarter, review your closed tickets to identify where you are spending significant time on rote or repeat tasks. Use your Salesforce superpowers to reduce your workload.

Real-Life Examples

Having fewer routine tasks means more time for building value-add solutions. Plus, it makes your work life more fun! Here are a few examples of how some awesome admins I've been fortunate to work with have leveraged their Salesforce admin skills to decrease ticket volume.

- **Created a flow** on a custom object used for tracking job titles, which automatically added a new user with the required role, profile, and permissions, and then sent a welcome email. This solution allowed the team to outsource the user set-up process to the service desk without needing to provide that team Sys Admin credentials.

- **Deployed a Dataloader.io Lightning app** so users could self-serve routine data loads using pre-defined data map templates and their existing user permissions, removing the risk of data-load debacles. This initiative required a little help from the Dev team, but the payoff was worth it, as the solution eliminated dozens of data loads a week!

- **Built screen-flow "wizards"** so Super Users could change field values and delete records to address common user-error scenarios that previously required Salesforce admin intervention.

- **Added a field** to track the number of so-called issues that were actually gaps in training or business process knowledge. Armed with this data, they convinced the business unit to appoint someone to address these tickets, providing more time for Salesforce admins to work on the platform activities they are uniquely qualified to do.

Establish a Deployment Schedule

You may work in an organization with a stringent policy around the deployment process. If that is the case, I hope you have enough flexibility to develop and deploy solutions incrementally. Conversely, you may work in an organization where deployments, or what you call a release or rollout, happen anytime and all the time, whenever changes are requested. To ensure that we are all on the same page when referring to deployments, I'm referring to the changes you make to the system infrastructure or metadata through the Setup menu. Deployments might include adding a field, tweaking existing fields, introducing a validation rule, or automating a process with a flow. These changes should never be done directly in production. They should be thoroughly tested in a sandbox to ensure that everything is working correctly and that you've identified all unintended consequences. Deployments do not include those items I call admin tasks, generally done in real time as needed. These include adding users, sharing reports, assigning permission sets, doing data loads, and executing other day-to-day administrative functions that don't fundamentally alter the infrastructure.

Assuming that deployment schedules are something you can influence in your organization, I encourage you to get your stakeholders accustomed to a regularly scheduled deployment cadence as an effective calm-the-chaos technique. Your release cadence can be weekly, bi-weekly, or monthly, depending on the appetite for change in your company and the scope of your typical release size. Be sure to communicate that this is the standard policy. It's best not to wait too long before implementing minor enhancements, so you might even have a weekly release for these and a monthly or quarterly release for more-significant changes.

If you work with multiple user groups, you might stagger your release cadence for each team. In other words, you might communicate to Sales that you release changes on the first and third week of the month and convey to Customer Support that you release mid-month.

Why is communicating a release schedule a good thing? More importantly, how does it help you cut the chaos?

- It forces stakeholder discipline and removes a false sense of urgency. They will know there is a process for making changes, so you don't have to be the villain when you refuse to update on demand.

- It allows ample time for both testing and documentation.

- It provides time to develop user communications.

- It ensures that you don't find yourself doing post-production support every morning or working late every night to push production changes.

- It assures your stakeholders that there is already another release date on the schedule when you suggest deploying their changes incrementally.

Sticking to set release schedules will help you calm the chaos, but there may be times when you need to make exceptions for your sake. Assuming that you follow your company's change-control policies, use your judgment if something makes sense to deploy in between releases, particularly if it benefits you. As an example, if you need to add a true/false field to facilitate a reporting requirement to finish a dashboard you're working on for a stakeholder, don't wait a week, especially if it's innocuous and behind the scenes, and it allows you to get an outstanding deliverable over the finish line. The intent is to establish a policy that benefits, not hinders, you.

 Pro tip: You can design the policy to accommodate exceptions, but I encourage you to require a few extra steps when off-cycle releases are requested, such as an email with the business justification or written approval from a business unit leader. You will be amazed by how many things aren't so urgent after all when someone besides you has an action item.

 ## TALK TRACKS:

Communicating a Release Cadence

➢ After reviewing your requested changes, we can include the two new fields in this week's release. The other modifications warrant more time to execute and test, so we'll include those in the mid-month release.

➢ I understand that these changes are critical. Our next regular release is scheduled for two weeks from Friday. I can probably accommodate the request, but I'll need to circulate an approval for an out-of-cycle release. To facilitate that, please shoot me an email explaining why it's time-sensitive so I can initiate that process.

Define a Warranty Period

When I introduced the minimum viable product (MVP) concept in Chapter 7, you heard about how common it is to get change requests immediately after deploying something new. In some cases, this will be due to discovering an edge case, one of those once-in-a-while scenarios that no one thought to consider. In other cases, a step may have been missed during the deployment such that something working correctly in your sandbox acts wonky in production. Alternatively, your stakeholders could have a slight change of heart once they see their users interacting with the system's new functionality. You may hear something like, "We thought it would be better to remove that field from the page, but the team insists they need that data point." No matter how thorough you were in understanding requirements, building the solution, and testing it, tweaks will be needed and changes will be requested, so you may as well plan accordingly.

Consider implementing a time-boxed warranty period with an agreed-on set of rules regarding immediate post–go live support and a timeline for revisiting how the functionality is working in the days or weeks after deployment. There is no one-size-fits-all approach, as the number of days for each part is relative to the scope and must make sense as part of your overall support and enhancement strategy.

By defining in advance what Salesforce admin support looks like during each stage of the warranty period, your stakeholders will know what to expect. They will have peace of mind that they will get assistance as needed, and they will appreciate that you have time set aside to iterate and improve, which is an integral part of getting them to agree to an MVP approach. Equally important, a defined warranty period sets the expectation with your stakeholders that even though you will provide an elevated level of support immediately following a release, this is not your standard operating procedure. Nor do they get to keep coming back indefinitely for just-in-time tweaks and changes. Getting your stakeholders comfortable with the concept will make it easier for you to reinforce that they need to go to the back of the line when they have future requests. Changes outside the defined warranty period require the usual intake and prioritization process.

The initial warranty period. When implementing new functionality, it's essential to be available for just-in-time support if something's not working as intended. Generally speaking, this refers to the hours immediately after the release or when users start logging in, when you provide an elevated level of support, sometimes referred to as hypercare. Any new functionality not working or acting differently than expected should get fixed as quickly as possible. Additionally, it's not uncommon for your business partners to request configuration tweaks based on immediate user feedback. These typically include minor adjustments to page layouts, adding fields to reports, modifying dashboard widgets, and completing other quick hits that improve the process or user experience without fundamentally impacting how things work. Define which types of changes you will address as initial warranty items and agree to prioritize and execute these as quickly as possible to ensure a smooth deployment.

The extended warranty period. The timeline for this will vary depending on the nature of the change. Generally, this kicks in after the first few days, or perhaps the first week after the deployment, and may run for several weeks. The extended warranty period is when you will address missed requirements and edge cases that emerge and tackle things that aren't working as smoothly as they should be. These changes warrant more consideration and take longer than the just-in-time tweaks described above. Ideally, you'll watch the new process for some agreed time and then review and prioritize a list of stories with your business partner. You will likely agree that some items, especially straightforward ones or those fixing material defects, warrant a near-term rollout. You will probably also identify nice-to-have changes to add to your backlog and execute as time permits.

Fast-follow release(s). You'll schedule subsequent deployments for items that do not require immediate action. These might include requirements identified as out of scope for MVP and things that come up as incremental improvements when users start interacting with the system. I encourage you to plan cycles to address these as quickly as possible, as this goes a long way toward getting your stakeholders comfortable with an iterative approach.

Pro tip: During the initial warranty period, I make a slight exception to my requirement that all change requests and production bugs be submitted through the ticketing process. Due to the just-in-time nature of post-deployment troubleshooting and the fact that many so-called bugs often turn out to be erroneously reported, I set up a shared spreadsheet for tracking issues. Any issues that require system work still get entered as tickets, but the spreadsheet provides an easy way to collaborate immediately after a release. If you go this route, it's important to communicate with your stakeholders that it's a temporary tracking process for immediate launch issues only. Be sure to tell them when to stop using it, assuring them that you have moved all open items to your standard ticketing system.

DOS AND DON'TS FOR THE WARRANTY PERIOD

- **Do** incorporate the warranty period in your change management or deployment policy so all parties agree on the approach, including your change committee or internal audit team. Even just-in-time changes should go through the standard testing, approval, and deployment process.

- **Do** clarify with your stakeholders how you will communicate about issues immediately after a launch. Should they follow the standard ticket submission process? Will you have a live chat available the morning after the deployment for real-time collaboration?

- **Do** block time on your schedule to account for the initial warranty period the morning after a deployment.

- **Do** assume you'll need to plan ongoing enhancements through the extended warranty period. From a capacity standpoint, you are not finished with that workstream until you wrap up that post-deployment support, so consider that when providing estimates or communicating your availability to begin new initiatives.

- **Don't** plan a major project or significant release immediately after another one. If something goes wrong or takes longer than planned, you'll be glad you gave yourself a time cushion.

TALK TRACKS:

Setting Stakeholder Expectations During and After the Warranty Period

➤ As part of the initial warranty process, I've addressed the issues with field-level security and added the list view you requested. The other items fall more into the category of an enhancement request, which we'll prioritize once we move into the extended warranty phase.

➤ As a reminder, we have stabilized all deployment issues and transitioned to the extended warranty period. If there's a showstopper, let me know right away. Otherwise, please maintain a list of any feedback or desired enhancements, and we'll meet on Monday to review and establish a plan of attack.

➤ I love your enthusiasm for improving the functionality we released last month. We deployed a great solution and made it even better with the changes made during the warranty period. Since that has ended, the process now is to enter any additional enhancement requests through our standard ticketing system. We can schedule a monthly meeting to review and prioritize to ensure we continue to iterate and improve.

Conduct an Initial Consult

"We'd like to discuss extending our use of Salesforce to the Delivery team."

"We need to start automating all the communications we send."

"We're thinking about using Salesforce to standardize our approval process."

Do these types of requests sound familiar? In addition to the more rote tickets that come through your queue, your business partners will inevitably reach out to discuss significant enhancements or new functionality they want to add. These requests could entail bringing on a new group of users, adding new features, automating a new business process, or any combination. Before the request formally comes in, as soon as you get wind that something is brewing, schedule a brief "initial consult" (15–30 minutes max).

What is an initial consult? And why bother talking about things that aren't yet on the to-do list? This discussion is similar to an initial meeting you might have with a doctor, lawyer, or other service provider. The intent is not to get into the nitty-gritty requirements or provide solutions but to understand at a high level what your business partners are trying to accomplish to determine 1) whether Salesforce is an appropriate solution, 2) whether the request is feasible given the size, scope, and availability of resources, and 3) whether the requester has identified and addressed any dependencies and prerequisites. This conversation not only allows you to provide value but benefits you.

Here are typical outcomes for an initial consult:

- **The request is redundant** with something that's already on the docket. If so, you've added value by connecting the stakeholders, ensuring alignment, and eliminating duplicate efforts.

- **The ask makes no sense for Salesforce** due to its complexity or other reasons. If so, you've added value by providing expert advice and saving time and effort.

- **The request requires significant prework** or has dependencies. If so, you've added value by calling out these action items so that others can work on them in advance, improving overall project velocity.

- **The ask is much less complicated** than anticipated, which is not uncommon when working with business partners who may be unfamiliar with the platform's configuration capabilities. I can't tell you how often I've engaged in an initial discussion, having been forewarned that I should be prepared for some pretty heavy asks, only to receive Salesforce 101 requirements. If this is the case, you can move the request into your standard intake process to prioritize and address as part of your BAU activities, adding value by delivering in less time and with less investment than anticipated.

- **The ask is much more complicated** than anticipated, allowing for discussions about adequate resourcing, budgets, and project planning.

Short initial meetings can help the business stakeholder determine if their proposed request is technically feasible and suited for Salesforce, understand the approximate level of effort, and sometimes even get the project off your to-do list. Done right, over time, your colleagues will value your input and judgment and get in the habit of looping you in at the early stage. I consider these outcomes an excellent return on investment for a short meeting, but I encourage you to keep the ground rules in mind.

DOS AND DON'TS FOR AN INITIAL CONSULT

- **Do** clarify the objective upfront and call time out if you start getting into the nitty-gritty requirements.

- **Do** clarify that any estimates you provide are preliminary pending the actual requirements session. You can avoid providing a specific estimate while still giving context. Is it something you expect you could address as part of your BAU activities? Is it a large enough initiative that warrants treatment as a significant project? Will it require outside resources?

- **Do** specify any information or deliverables you would need to engage. Recommend homework your business partners can initiate to get started, such as documenting a business process flow, answering a list of questions, or defining logic for a conditional workflow.

- **Don't** forget to explore the potential impact this initiative might have on you or others on the Salesforce team. Will this increase the number of users in the system? Will it increase the complexity of the system? Will it materially increase your ongoing support tasks? If so, you have an opportunity to raise this as an issue in advance to ensure that the initiative can be appropriately resourced and supported.

Create a Mutual Plan

This particular technique will be overkill for the small BAU tickets that come into your queue, but consider it an essential calm-the-chaos strategy for any sizeable request, such as a significant enhancement or rollout of net-new functionality. Most top-performing sales organizations have some concept of a mutual plan as a component of their sales playbook, so this will likely be familiar to Sales Cloud admins.

A mutual plan is a written document that helps the sales team and prospect partner ensure that both parties know their responsibilities throughout the buying journey. It prevents the sales rep from spinning their wheels with an unqualified prospect, which becomes evident if said prospect does not meet their commitments at preordained checkpoints. Sales reps leverage the mutual plan to create trust, joint accountability, and partnership.

For Salesforce admins, a mutual plan provides a mechanism for aligning responsibilities, setting expectations, and ensuring a better experience for all parties involved. It reinforces the message that automating business processes and implementing new features requires collaboration. You can't do it alone. A mutual plan allows you to document and assign action owners to all the necessary steps on the business and technical fronts. This approach adds specificity to the work at hand, including critical milestones, and clarifies the level of involvement required from each team. You can use it to document the activities in which your stakeholders must be willing and able to participate. The more specific you can be, like including dates and times, the better, but you don't have to wait until you know all the details to start the discussion.

Review the plan at a high level as early as possible to ensure that they are willing to commit the required time and resources, and then you can continue to add color as the project progresses. If you sense any hesitation in accepting the action items, you have a few options. You might agree to take on more, assuming that the additional tasks you take are appropriate for your role and that you have the available bandwidth or can negotiate trade-offs as needed. You can explore whether other colleagues could pick up some of the pieces. Or, you can candidly suggest that there may be a better time to engage when they have the appropriate time to dedicate to the project to ensure its success. If stakeholder cooperation or availability is going to be an issue, you benefit by surfacing these issues well before starting an initiative.

So, why should you create a mutual plan? What's in it for you?

- It lays out precisely what's needed from all parties, so there are no surprises

- It takes you off the hook as the sole person responsible for getting the project executed

- It defines checkpoints that will save you time if your business partner is not meeting their commitments; if they aren't hustling for their own project, why should you?

SAMPLE ACTION ITEMS YOU MIGHT ASSIGN TO YOUR BUSINESS PARTNER IN A MUTUAL PLAN

✓ Documentation of the current state process

✓ Collection of existing reports to show how the process is currently managed

✓ Participation in a half-day requirements workshop to document the future state

✓ Being available for hourly demo sessions as needed during the design process

✓ Participating in solution review sessions

✓ Assigning team members to return clean data in the template provided

✓ Allocating resources for user acceptance testing

✓ Development of communication materials

✓ Reviewing and signing off of training materials

✓ Ensuring that team members complete required training

✓ Assigning of resources as needed to assist with user questions or issues during and after the deployment

✓ Being available to review deployment results and enhancement requests at each transition stage in the warranty period

✓ Being responsible for ongoing data quality and monitoring of process compliance

 Pro tip: Your mutual plan shouldn't end at deployment. As in sales, where the real trick is agreeing on how the client will be successful after the deal is closed, it's essential to plan how the new features or functionality will be supported. Leverage the mutual plan to specify who's responsible for activities such as training new users or reviewing data to ensure record completeness and accuracy. Document predetermined milestones when you agree to review enhancement requests or deploy additional functionality.

 Pro tip: When you identify significant potential workstreams, don't leave the meeting with yourself having all the action items. It's easy for stakeholders to want it all and enthusiastically nod when you are solely on point for moving forward. When you share the onus with them, you'll often find that the level of urgency declines dramatically.

CHAPTER 12:

TECHNIQUES TO REDUCE THE OVERWHELM

If Mama ain't happy, ain't nobody happy.

—Unknown

Your success as a Salesforce admin is not defined only by the needs of your stakeholders. Like all relationships, it needs to be a two-way street. To shine as the problem-solving, proactive, value-adding resource you are, you need the time, space, and brainpower to work your magic without things coming at you like you're working the window at McAdmin's Drive-Thru. Adding value is possible only when you have a reasonable amount of work and realistic deadlines based on what else is on your plate.

We've already established that the more value you provide, the faster the demands will come flying at you. Your reputation precedes you. People want what you've got and know what you can do for them. If you don't set limits, your stakeholders will keep pushing for more. It's not necessarily intentional, but they'll keep moving the bar. Now they need it faster. And you are suddenly working more late nights and can't keep all the balls in the air. It can be a slippery slope.

I get it. It feels good to swoop in as a Salesforce admin superhero and save the day. Still, saving the day and being a hero with a whole night's sleep feels even better. Or, better yet, imagine how good you would feel if you always had sufficient timelines and resources such that personal heroics were no longer required.

This chapter introduces five techniques that will help make that a reality. These will help ensure a reasonable workload without alienating or infuriating your stakeholders. They'll allow you to leverage your Salesforce superhero street cred to deftly push back, slow down, reset, and get help when needed.

Provide Realistic Timelines

One of the more common complaints I hear from Salesforce admins is that there's too much to do and not enough hours in the day to get it done. As we look at ways to work with our stakeholders to create more sustainable workloads and turnaround times, we must first address a foundational issue prevalent among Salesforce admins: underestimating the amount of time or effort required. Yep, it's often our own fault that we're so darn busy!

Guess who said that the functionality could be live in two weeks? Guess who committed to have that new report, including all those summary calculations, tomorrow? Guess who indicated that those changes were easy, so completing them before the sales meeting would be no problem? *You did!*

You probably said it would be easy breezy because the hands-on-keyboard work would be. Unless, of course, you hit a snag or start drilling in and realizing there's something tangly in the data model.

Furthermore, did you consider all the work already on your plate that may prevent you from sitting down to work on the request? Did you account for the likelihood of being interrupted with hair-on-fire requests, that you may need to take a sick day, that you may get an error when you try to push to production, or whatever else may come up? Did you bake in time for thorough testing, documentation, deployment across multiple environments, and any required release communications?

Underestimating the level of effort and tasks required to get a change over the finish line is a major chaos-causing culprit, often necessitating work on weekends and evenings to catch up. Missing deadlines because you underestimated the work can negatively impact your otherwise stellar reputation and disappoint the raving fan base you worked so hard to obtain. The good news is that it's not just Salesforce admins who consistently underestimate how long something takes to do. There's a lot of science behind this very human tendency, which means there are also some specific ways to improve.

Who knew it was a thing? There's a name for it!

In 1979, social scientists Daniel Kahneman and Amos Tversky coined the term Planning Fallacy, which refers to an optimistic prediction bias in which people underestimate the time it will take them to complete a task despite knowing that similar tasks have typically taken them much longer. The team observed that as people consider how long something will take, they usually fail to account for the fact that they will likely encounter unexpected obstacles, delays, and interruptions. (You never have any of those, right?)

Kahneman expanded on their original idea years later, explaining that estimation mistakes are generally twofold. First, there's a failure to consider how long it's taken to complete similar tasks in the past, and second, there's an assumption that there will be no complications that cause delays, which he termed Optimism Bias.

As if being the poster child for Planning Fallacy and Optimism Bias isn't enough for Salesforce admin types to contend with, other research indicates that divided attention, a fairly constant state for Salesforce admins, also makes it harder for us to estimate project length. We forget to account for switching costs, which is the toll on time and brainpower when multi-tasking or performing two or more tasks in rapid succession, compounded delays, and needing breaks between tasks.

The Estimate Equation

To break this cycle and provide more accurate estimates, we must account for the inevitable hiccups, assume there will be some hurdles and delays, and acknowledge that it's unlikely we'll be able to knock something out from start to finish without numerous interruptions. We also need to be realistic about the steps involved in deploying changes. Let's put that in Salesforce terms using a formula to help you do that and then dig into the components of the equation, including how each adds time to your task.

There are two buckets of time with any task. First there's the actual time it takes to do the work. For the Salesforce admin, this includes everything from researching possible approaches to the actual hands-on-keyboards work, including configuration, testing, creating a change set, pushing it from a sandbox into production, and all the steps in between. (For our purposes, let's assume you've already done the work to validate the request and confirm what problem you're solving.) You could use a stopwatch to capture the amount of time spent on each of these activities and calculate the time it takes to execute the work.

The second bucket is the elapsed time from receiving the request until your solution is live. Your stopwatch may clock only 90 minutes for total work time, but suppose you don't have time to get started for a week. Or, say you keep getting interrupted and can't get through an activity without many stops and starts. The elapsed time until you can deliver the work is suddenly much longer than 90 minutes. To get to a more realistic estimate, you'll want to account for both buckets of time, the items we often gloss over, plus all the unexpected things.

THE ESTIMATE EQUATION

Estimated Time to Completion = The Time it Takes + When You Can Start + The Gotchas + The Law of Unintended Consequences + Data Fun + Testing + Deployment Activities + Documentation + Switching Costs + the Fire Drill Factor + Padding the Bill

If that seems like a long equation for simple Salesforce changes, that's exactly the point! Let's look at the additional components in detail.

Assume You'll Have Gotchas

Suppose you need to make a simple, straightforward configuration change, so you commit to a quick turn-around time. For instance, you need to add a formula field to the Opportunity object or send an email to the assigned CSR manager at a point in the case-management process. These fall into what I consider the quick-hit category. That is, until they don't! It's smooth sailing until you hit a Salesforce platform limit or unexpected configuration challenge that adds time or complexity.

Typical Salesforce Gotchas

- **Hitting system limitations** such as the number of custom lookup fields you can have on an object or the number of actions you can have on an Approval step.

- **Getting the Relationship Spanning Limit error.** Unlike the system limits explicitly visible on each custom object, there's no way to see that you're nearing this limit until you try to add a field and get the message that you're out of luck. (Hint: You can log a case with Salesforce Support to increase.)

- **Trying to save your formula** and getting the dreaded Compilation Size error message. This one can be a head-scratcher the first time you see it, as the formula may be very simple, but if it references other complex formulas that total more than the allotted character limit, you'll get a syntax error.

- **Discovering that the email address** you need for your email alert resides in a formula field that isn't available when selecting the recipient.

- **Stumbling into random limitations** on standard objects, such as the fact that you can't have related lists on the User object or field-history tracking on Activities.

If you've been doing Salesforce for a while, you've probably hit all these roadblocks and then some. The takeaway is that these types of gotchas are not an exception to the rule. They're standard fare that you'll frequently encounter when solutioning, particularly as you start adding more complexity to an org, so you should always build in some contingency time.

Beware the Law of Unintended Consequences

Just when you think you've escaped all the gotchas, you risk running into the Law of Unintended Consequences. This covers all sorts of results that could follow your making a seemingly innocuous change. For example, you suddenly see existing automation errors because your change was the tipping point for SOQL limits. Or that simple validation rule you need to add now necessitates changes to multiple test classes to prevent deployment errors.

Unintended consequences may include process impacts in addition to system impacts. For instance, the field label changes the sales VP requested to match the new selling vernacular means you need to change many dashboard titles, help hovers, email alert templates, and other references to that field.

Don't Discount the Data

If the task at hand has anything to do with migrating or importing data, assume added complexity and time. I learned early in my career that the work it takes to get a file ready for import can take on a life of its own, particularly when you need to map unstructured data into structured fields across multiple objects. If pressed, you can provide an estimate for the rest of the work with a commitment to provide an estimate for data prep once you determine the state of the data. A few tips:

- Provide context to explain the activities required before loading any data into the system. Include examples such as formatting date and time values, ensuring that restricted picklists don't prohibit cell values, and using VLOOKUPS to associate the data with existing records.

- Don't assume you need to be the one to fix all the issues. If you can be very specific about the problems in the file, the requestor may be willing and able to own this. While this will free you up for other work, there may be delays in the time it takes for them to get the data back to you, so consider that in your timeline.

- Plan for multiple iterations. Sometimes a data file will error out due to one issue, and once you've addressed that and re-try the upload, you'll see different errors on the second pass.

Testing & Deployment Activities

You need time to test your work. Ideally, there's always a second set of eyes. At a minimum, the requestor should review your change in the sandbox. Don't forget about creating a report or monitoring dashboard as applicable to ensure sure things are working as expected. And then there's the deployment itself, which includes moving your changes from one or more sandboxes into production.

Documentation

Even minor config changes require some amount of documentation and deployment time. At a minimum, you need to document in your story or ticket the work done. You may need to update a description field or data dictionary. You may need to fill out a change request for audit purposes.

Switching Costs and the Fire-Drill Factor

The ideal way to get a job done is to block chunks of time on your calendar and turn off email notifications so you can complete a task from start to finish and work without distractions. If that's not realistic in your world, you must account for the switching costs accordingly. Similarly, if your job regularly includes hair-on-fire interruptions when you must drop everything, you need to account for that.

So How Long Should We Say It's Going to Take?

Repeat after me: *It always takes longer than you think.*

Here are three things you can do to create more realistic timeframes:

- **Practice not providing an estimate** until you've had time to do initial research. Get comfortable not committing to a timeline until you thoroughly review the request. It's okay to acknowledge that you don't yet know how long it will take.

- **If data is involved, always add a caveat** that data prep time will vary based on the state of the data and who will be responsible for remediation.

- **Take a moment to consider all the inputs and unknowns in the estimate equation** and start padding the proverbial bill. As a rule of thumb, start by multiplying your initial estimate by three.

Adding that much time to your estimate may feel like overkill if you're accustomed to delivering fast time to value, but it's a skill you need to borrow from our friends in the consulting world. Consulting fees are generally based on time and materials, so when providing an estimate, consultants are incented and trained to carefully consider every hour they might spend executing a project.

Raise your hand if you've ever seen an estimate from an external implementation partner and found it full of fluff. *Forty hours for some simple automation? I could knock that out in a day!* Maybe you could if you could guarantee no interruptions or unexpected challenges, or perhaps if you didn't have to document your work and then move it across multiple sandboxes. But that's not reality. Instead, let's take a lesson from the consulting playbook and factor these things into our timelines.

As you start being mindful of each component in the equation, you'll begin creating more-realistic estimates. When referring to the time required for lightweight lifts, a colleague used to say, "It's still bigger than zero." Even when you're making small changes, many still-bigger-than-zero items can quickly add up!

When you start paying attention to your initial assessment and tracking it against how things actually play out, you'll become more accustomed to considering these elements. Over time, you may not need this trick, or you may determine your own time-length multiplier that will get you pretty darn close.

CAUTION! A CALM-THE-CHAOS CAVEAT

If you've been historically low in your estimates and have been compensating with long hours to meet your deadlines, you may have set a precedent with your stakeholders, who've subsequently come to expect unrealistic turnaround times. They may push back the first time you present a more realistic estimate: "*A week!* You did this last time in a day." You can explain that you've been tracking time to task and that the data, coupled with the fact that you're adding rigor around documentation and testing to provide improved quality and system sustainability, warrants timelines that better match the work involved. When you've proven to be a value-adding resource, they'll trust that you're providing honest estimates based on empirical data and grant you the time you need to deliver quality work.

Pro tip: When we say we're going to do something by a certain date, we need to honor our commitment. However, if it turns out that it's simply not feasible due to complexity or volume or some change in circumstances, your responsibility is not to pull a bunch of all-nighters to make it happen. Your responsibility is to communicate the issue *as soon as possible* and align on reducing scope, adding resources, or adjusting the deadline accordingly.

DOS AND DON'TS
FOR PROVIDING REALISTIC TIMELINES

- **Do** delay making timeline commitments until you've had ample time to assess the work.

- **Do** consider including a confidence level for your planned dates. If you go this route, commit to a date when you'll provide a more firm timeline.

- **Do** phone a colleague or friend for a gut check.

- **Do** estimate during the low point of your day, not when you're bright-eyed and ready to rock after a relaxing weekend, as you'll likely create more realistic estimates.

- **Do** track your time. It can be tedious, but even if you do it for only 30 days, you'll likely have enough empirical evidence to get comfortable increasing your estimates.

- **Don't** make any firm commitments regarding a data file you haven't had a chance to review.

TALK TRACKS:

Communicating Timelines

➤ This seems straightforward, but I need to check for system implications and run it up against what's in the queue to see when I can realistically get to this. How about if I get back to you by Friday with a level of effort and approximate time frame?

➤ Based on what I know right now, I estimate this will take about two days to do the work. Realistically, I won't have a chance to look at it until the middle of next week, so we could plan to review it next Friday. Once I get started, I'll let you know if I encounter anything that will impact the timeline.

➤ Based on my current understanding, I'm 50% confident I can get to this by the end of the month. I can provide a more firm timeline by next Friday. How does that sound?

Trade-Offs Are the Currency of Calm

I've mentioned trade-offs throughout this book, but we are about to take a deep dive. Consider your available time and attention as sitting in two containers. When these containers are full, you must remove something to add more. In other words, the answer to every ask cannot be yes. It's not sustainable, nor is it realistic. Something has to give. Eventually, it will either be you or the quality of your work. You'll be exhausted and overwhelmed or find yourself in situations where you can't meet your commitments and deadlines, eroding all those value points you worked so hard to put on the board.

In the Salesforce admin world, trade-offs are the give-and-takes required to ensure you can get through the highest value requests without working 24/7. They are your superhero cape, bullet-defying bracelets, and invisible shield. Go forth without them at your peril.

Trade-offs are the missing link between calm and chaos. They are powerful because they prevent you from saying yes when it's not reasonable or feasible. Instead of saying no—a word that can be hard to say and hard for stakeholders to hear—trade-offs instead convey "Yes, but…."

"Yes, I can do that. Yes, I can meet that timeline. Yes, but…."

And here's the important message to convey: "Something has to give to make it happen."

Here are trade-offs I encourage you to consider as needed when you get new requests. In each situation, some or all of these may apply.

FOUR TYPES OF TRADE-OFFS

You can meet the request but you need more resources.

 TALK TRACK:

> ➤ To get all of this into production on Tuesday instead of Thursday, I will need people from your team to help get the data in the correct format before we can load the files. Do you have resources who can assist?

You can meet the request but you need more time.

 TALK TRACK:

> ➤ We can include the additional items, but they require code and QA, adding at least a week to our planned go-live date. Would you like to adjust the timetable, or would you prefer to add that part of the request to the backlog?

You can meet the timeline but will have to delay something else.

 TALK TRACK:

> ➤ I can make all the requested changes and still meet tomorrow's deployment deadline, but if I do that, I won't be able to finish building the new dashboard. If I have time for only one of these tasks, which would you prefer I complete?

You can meet the timeline but you'll have to reduce the scope.

 TALK TRACK:

> ➤ I can include your request as part of this week's release if we agree to exclude the automated emails. How does that sound?

When you feel a trade-off is required, provide context as to why. Don't just lay out the options. Share the advantages and disadvantages as you see them.

This is where your expertise and POV come into play. For instance, sometimes bringing more people into an active workstream is more trouble than it's worth. By the time the additional workers get up to speed and start adding value, the opportunity cost of the time and attention it took from you may cancel out the benefit. Other times, an extra person may be just the ticket. Lead with your POV. Given the request, do you think it's best to adjust the timeline? Or do you think it's best to deploy and add the new features in a follow-up release? Recommend what you think makes sense given your knowledge of resource constraints, business priorities, and any potential impact on your users.

Even though trade-offs are critical for calming chaos, most Salesforce admins I know aren't good at asking for them. Perhaps as a Salesforce admin community, we need to spend more time talking about the concept. We also may not realize we need a trade-off until it's too late. It's hard to ask for help or negotiate a trade-off at 7 p.m. when we finally comprehend the unruly state of the data we said we could upload by morning, which is why it's so important to review the data before committing to a timeline.

The work can creep in rather sneakily. There's not necessarily one major thing that warrants a trade-off discussion. Instead, we experience the proverbial death by a thousand paper cuts. Every item we deal with turns out to be a tad bigger, messier, or more complex than anticipated. In this case, the cumulative effect may warrant a prioritization or trade-off discussion.

Pro tip: When you initiate a task and then determine that it's more complex or time-consuming than you anticipated, it's perfectly reasonable to go back to your stakeholder or boss and ask for a trade-off. Ideally, you can refrain from providing a definite turn-around time until you have all the facts or at least set the expectation that you may have to revisit an estimated timeline once you start doing the work. Either way, you are entitled to renegotiate timelines and resources once you have a complete picture of what is required. Get comfortable stating "Now that I understand what this will require…" and following that with whatever trade-off you want to propose.

Scope Creep Does Not Get a Free Pass

Scope creep refers to an increase in requirements, such as when a single deliverable suddenly multiplies or when a project objective expands beyond what you originally agreed to do. For example, let's say you agreed to create a couple of reports to support an initiative, but in the course of the discussion, your stakeholder decides that to achieve the desired goal, they need a dashboard, automated email reminders, *and* a new custom object.

Scope creep is rarely someone's intention, and more importantly, it's not inherently bad. In the discovery process, you will often find technical dependencies or realize that business needs require something bigger or more complicated than initially requested. This is common in technology projects. Since it's critical to deliver the right solution, good project managers will raise the issue and expand timelines and resources accordingly.

Scope creep is often more subtle and insidious for Salesforce admins. Extra work piles on in such a way that you don't realize it's even happening. On the Salesforce platform, the art of the possible is often much more robust than anyone envisioned, so requests that started small take on a life of their own once you and your business partner start digging into how the platform can help.

Before we get into strategies for dealing with scope creep, here's a little secret that may hit home: Salesforce admins are frequently complicit in expanding the scope. Yep, let's face it. Those extra features are often *your* idea!

When you roll up your sleeves and get into the weeds with your stakeholders to augment an existing process or stand up something new, you're in the zone. Your gears start grinding on what else is possible and how else you can leverage the platform. The next thing you know, you suddenly have ideas about all sorts of things you can or should solve. Plus, you inevitably uncover edge cases to address, gaps where validation rules or automation are necessary to enforce a step in the process, or downstream impacts on something seemingly unrelated.

Delivering the right thing is essential, and creating value by helping your stakeholders maximize the platform is what Salesforce is all about. However, when there was no expectation that it was bigger than a breadbox and now it suddenly is, you must acknowledge that and adjust. When the scope expands, your timeline or resource allocations must change too. Ideally, you can break the work into small, manageable chunks with your business partner's agreement on what constitutes the minimum viable product that will suffice for the first release. Alternatively, if you don't pare back the scope, something else in your queue must officially be delayed. Otherwise, while the end result may create tremendous value, scope creep means that one more heaping plate just landed on your already full stack. Scope creep is how late nights, weekend work, and overwhelm happen, and it often hits you a little at a time, so you don't notice it.

DOS AND DON'TS
WHEN SCOPE CREEP SNEAKS IN

- **Do** discuss whether the added deliverables are must-haves or nice-to-haves. If you confirm they're required for a complete solution and they'll add time or complexity to the project, review what's on your plate and propose the most appropriate trade-off.

- **Do** consider whether you can chunk out the elements of the ask into multiple releases. If you can sequence the new work into a separate workstream, make a recommendation to complete the original task as planned and schedule a meeting to discuss subsequent workstreams.

- **Do** recognize this is fairly common, and include wiggle room when providing estimated timelines. (Remember the estimate equation? Scope creep is part of the reason we always pad the bill.)

- **Don't** assume you must incorporate all last-minute feedback. If you're ready to go live and get a change or enhancement for something not mission-critical, put it in your backlog and agree to review it during the warranty period.

- **Don't** feel obligated to take on extra work without a trade-off just because the add-on was your idea. Bringing up great ideas or more robust solutions does not commit you to immediately delivering that functionality.

Say No in a Way that Gets You a Smile and a Thank You

Is saying no difficult for you? It is for me, and I'd venture to guess the same is true for most Salesforce admins. We love solving problems, automating processes, and rolling out cool stuff. We love making our users and stakeholders happy. "Sure, I can help! Yes, I can do that. Easy breezy!"

So it can be tough to say no, especially when the ask involves solving a problem you know you can knock out of the ballpark with your Salesforce bag of tricks. Difficulty saying no is undoubtedly why many great Salesforce admins end up overwhelmed with a massive queue of requests and too many late nights.

If you struggle with saying no, consider the opportunity cost of saying yes. Will another project slip? If so, what are the implications going to be? Who will the work impact? Will you make one stakeholder happy at the expense of another? Will there be implications for your personal time? Suppose it's another night of working after dinner instead of putting the kids to bed, finishing your book, or hitting the gym. How will you feel? Remember that striking the right work/life balance will enable you to continue to be productive over the long haul.

The processes we've covered so far will introduce more rigor into how your requests are reviewed and prioritized, giving you cover and reducing the number of times you need to provide a flat-out no to a stakeholder. Still, there will always be one-off requests that, for whatever reason, aren't the right thing for you to be working on, or at least working on in the period requested, so it's essential to hone this skill.

Here are five suggestions to make it easier for you to say no in a way that allows you to maintain your Salesforce superhero cape.

- **Educate your constituents** to help them understand why some seemingly effortless things are complicated. Explain the constraints, complexity, and challenges that warrant the no.

- **Listen to the ask** and even if you believe your answer will need to be no, use your probing skills to understand what's behind it. Active listening is a win-win, as it cements your relationship with your business partners and ensures that you understand the scope of the request.

- **Instead of no, respond with "Yes, but…"** and clarify what trade-offs you would require. You might identify something else that can be pushed or agree that you can do the work on a different timetable than initially requested.

- **Put it in your backlog.** Type it up and send the link to your stakeholder with an indication of when it will be reviewed and prioritized.

- **Throw 'em a bone.** If the ask is too large to take on, see if you can identify things to keep the team moving forward until you can engage. A few examples:

  ✓ Conduct an initial consult

✓ Identify AppExchange applications they can investigate

✓ Provide reports that may help them identify a problem or assess a solution

✓ Leverage your Salesforce account team to do the required due diligence and provide product demos

TALK TRACKS:

Saying No

➤ I cannot take that on right now, but here are things I can do in the interim that may help you move forward.

➤ I'm not sure if this is feasible given my current workload. Let me review what's involved and I'll get back to you this afternoon.

Pro tip: If you need time to explore the ask, be clear on when you'll provide an answer. Respond as quickly as possible so there's no confusion that you have committed to the work and no delay on something important.

Throw the Flag when Needed

Throwing the flag means bringing awareness to an issue. Sometimes you may need assistance solving that issue. Other times, you may only need awareness from your boss or stakeholders to eliminate surprises or alert them to potential risks in the workstream. Raising issues or escalating problems doesn't feel as good as pushing shiny new functionality over the finish line, but throwing the proverbial flag when needed is the sign of a Salesforce admin pro. It's how not to get stuck in quicksand without anyone around to pull you out.

Let's look at a few examples of when raising an issue may be warranted.

The Work Is More Complex or Larger than You Can Handle

Despite your Salesforce admin awesomeness, you are a mere mortal. Some requested projects or initiatives will be outside the scope of what you can or should take on due to technical complexity or massive size. Suppose you've been asked to implement Salesforce CPQ to automate your company's pricing and proposals. Or you've been asked to implement a brand-new portal for your customers to log in on so they can interact directly with your account team. Yes, Salesforce admins can do this kind of work, but implementing significant new pieces of functionality may require a team that can focus on it without the distraction of a day job.

This is one of those times to remember that just because you *can* doesn't mean you *should*. Acknowledging that a project is more significant than you can or should handle does not make you a failure. You are responsible for educating your business partners and management team about what's feasible and ensuring that you don't kick off a project destined to fail. Consider this when you receive a significant request and reassess once you start digging into the requirements if the work is more than you can take on in addition to your current responsibilities.

Sometimes an ask seems reasonable and right in your wheelhouse until you figure out that it's much more complicated. Even though no code is the recommended starting place, sometimes code is a better route when there's significant automation or a high volume of records in play.

For example, suppose you get a request from your sales team to add automation to a new deal-qualification process. You ask all the right questions to confirm that you understand the why behind the ask and elicit a clear set of requirements that you believe you can quickly address. When you review the object to begin designing a solution, you see a veritable spaghetti of workflows, process builders, and code added over the years. This new request should be addressed in the context of a more extensive project to optimize the object. You throw the flag and recommend engaging with a developer to spend time analyzing and refactoring all of the object's automation. Yes, it will take longer. Yes, it may require development resources, but it's the right thing to do.

 Pro tip: Don't shy away from asking for additional resources just because you want the achievement of building something new on your resume. If you are lucky enough to work for a company willing to augment your team with additional resources when justified, use this as an opportunity to interact with and learn from other Salesforce professionals. Bringing in an external team doesn't mean you shouldn't play a pivotal project role. Display your ownership mindset and take responsibility to ensure the external team develops solutions that work in your org. Help plan the deployment such that your users will embrace the change and use the new functionality. Insist on knowledge transfer throughout the project and participate in the testing so you're well-positioned to support it.

Throw the Flag to Prevent Surprises

Sometimes throwing the flag is necessary to raise awareness of a potential issue and ensure that no one is caught off guard. There won't always be action needed, but you want to call attention to a potential problem. Your stakeholders and boss will appreciate the heads-up. No one likes surprises. Ensure that all stakeholders are looped in when there's a potential issue and gives them time to consider if and how they can mitigate the risk. Equally important, it provides cover for you. Once you throw the flag, the problem is no longer yours alone. When there are issues or potential issues, it's not only your responsibility to raise them; it's to your advantage so that others can help. It becomes up to your boss, the project manager, the committee, or everyone to help find a resolution.

Remember that employees and consultants rarely get dinged for asking for help, but they do get dinged for failing to report that help was needed. Throwing the flag is not a negative. It's a way to eliminate surprises and leverage others to mitigate issues so you don't have to go it alone.

A Real-Life Example

During a project integrating Salesforce with an ancillary financial system, I alerted my boss that I might need assistance. We had found a bug. The integration was not working as expected for certain records, but we couldn't immediately identify the root cause.

The business team insisted they still wanted to deploy because it seemed relatively limited in scope. They had committed to a deadline they didn't want to miss despite my insistence that the change wasn't ready for prime time.

I explained that we couldn't be sure of all the implications because we didn't know the root cause of the issue. What were the downstream impacts? How often were we going to see this error? Could we fix it if it came up in production? Given all the unknowns, there was no way I could deploy the changes.

I called my boss to let her know what was going on and confirm that she agreed with my conclusion. Giving her a heads-up meant she wouldn't be surprised and, equally important, would back me up if someone reached out to her about it. I then notified my primary business sponsor. (I worked remotely, or I would have had both conversations in person, as this type of discussion works best face to face when possible).

Ultimately, my stakeholders agreed that the risk of a production issue warranted a delay, and two days later, we successfully deployed without needing to hold our breath. Throwing the flag gave me the confidence that I would have support if I needed to escalate and ensured that my key stakeholder wasn't caught off guard when hearing the news from someone else that we'd pushed out the release date.

Pro tip: Another good reason to throw the flag is when you feel overwhelmed by all the work on your plate. Your boss can't help you prioritize or provide assistance when they don't know you're struggling.

Techniques in Action

Before we leave this chapter, let's take a moment to run through another hypothetical scenario to see some of these techniques in action, including how they work in conjunction with the Salesforce admin pro competencies we covered in the first part of this book.

Let's say you work for Jamal, who pops his head in your office to let you know that Cameron, the marketing director, will be reaching out to discuss a few system changes required in advance of a major new initiative that will be announced at the upcoming partner summit. "I think it's just a few fields and a new email template or something along those lines," he tells you. He says senior leadership is excited about this program, so he's hoping you can get those changes done in time.

"No problemo," you reply. "I'll connect with Cameron and see what she needs."

Uh-oh. You know where this is going. We've all been there. Sounds easy enough, so you say it would be no problem.

Jamal tells the leadership team it will be ready. Expectations have been set. Of course, no one knows what the "it" is or what "having it ready" entails. Maybe it really is just a few fields and an email template, but we've certainly seen that requests like this often turn into something entirely different once we figure out what problem they are trying to solve.

Avoid the Salesforce Admin Danger Zone

Warning! You are at risk of diving headfirst into the Salesforce admin danger zone. Without deliberate intervention, what you expected to be a calm week in which you could knock out some BAU tickets, finally catch up on org documentation, and finish that Salesforce Superbadge you've been working on will suddenly become a frenzy. Next thing you know, you'll find yourself smack in the middle of a bunch of late nights and crazy personal heroics to support this new initiative.

Let's rewind and see how you can employ some of the techniques we've covered, starting with the first conversation with Jamal when he tells you Cameron needs assistance. This time, resisting the urge to tell him it's no problem to get it done before you know what the work involves, you say, "I'm happy to give her a call today to understand exactly what is needed. Once I have that information, I'll loop back with you to confirm a timeline."

Excellent job setting expectations that you need to understand the ask before confirming when you can complete the task.

When you sit down with Cameron, instead of immediately diving into the mechanics of her requirements, you take a moment to see the bigger picture. "I understand we're kicking off a new initiative for our partners. Can you tell me more about that, including high-level objectives?"

Cameron walks you through the goals of the program and some related initiatives planned through the year, giving you needed context and some great ideas about how she might leverage the Salesforce platform for some of the future phases she's describing.

You're all about the value add, so you want to give her some food for thought before you dive into the topic at hand. "This is way out of scope for your immediate needs, but I want to make sure you're aware of some Salesforce capabilities that might be worth investigating later, given some of the outcomes you're looking to achieve."

You and Cameron have an animated conversation about the possibility of email campaigns, surveys, and perhaps an Experience Cloud site where the partners could log in and interact directly with the system. She had no idea that Salesforce offered such a broad range of solutions and is appreciative you brought these to her attention. Yes, these would all be fantastic use cases for the platform, but great ideas still qualify as scope creep when they aren't part of the original request. Most of these qualify as bigger-than-a-breadbox items that require prioritization and planning.

So, after a bit more brainstorming on the exciting ways Salesforce could support the new program, you propose tabling these topics. You set expectations with Cameron that these initiatives, particularly those requiring licensing costs or additional resources, will need to go to the steering committee to determine where they fit from a priority standpoint. Finally, you suggest she put some time on your calendar for an initial consult for a high-level discussion of potential costs, benefits, and levels of effort before any detailed planning.

Digging in to Understand the What and the When

Next, you don your BA hat and ask a series of questions to uncover what she's trying to accomplish in the near term to facilitate the program launch. Sure enough, the ask necessitates adding a few new fields, but as expected, you uncover that there's more involved in meeting her objectives. During the discussion, you determine that the initiative also warrants new reports, a new dashboard, and some automation to create a related record and initiate an approval process. Plus, she's got a data file she'd like you to use to upload values into the new fields for all the existing records.

"Jamal probably mentioned we'd like to introduce this at the upcoming partner event," she says. "How soon do you think you could have this done?"

Instead of immediately responding, you pose a question.

"When you say you want to *introduce this* at the partner event, what exactly does that mean?"

Great question! Maybe all of this doesn't have to be signed, sealed, and delivered with such a short turnaround time. Cameron confirms that having something to demo at the summit, even if it's not yet in production, would meet her needs. However, she encourages you to run that up the flag pole, given the senior leadership team's interest in it.

"So, how quickly could you have that ready?"

You've done a quick calculation and figured that if you spent the next two days working on it, you could probably knock it all out. Just as you're about to tell her that, you remember the estimate equation. You pause to think about how long it's been since you could work on one thing without interruption for an entire day, let alone two. You consider that the object requiring the automation already has a tremendous amount of workflow rules and process builders, plus a trigger. This object warrants an optimization project to streamline the automation and move it all to Flow, a project sitting in the backlog for months, so there's a chance you'll run up against the Law of Unintended Consequences. Plus, she mentioned a data load, but you haven't yet seen the file.

"I don't know. I need to do a little investigation, including reviewing your data file. I understand the urgency, so I'll get back to you tomorrow with a specific ETA."

Bingo! You've successfully avoided committing to a firm timeline until you can do your homework.

You give Jamal a heads up that the ask is bigger than expected, so you'll need to confirm priorities and discuss trade-offs to complete it in time for the summit.

Let's dive into how the conversation with Jamal might go.

First you share that you'd been planning to work on the documentation you committed to getting to him by the end of the week. You confirm that Cameron's request should take priority, which means the documentation won't be complete until sometime the following week. Jamal agrees that's the right priority. You then share Cameron's opinion that previewing the solution in a sandbox would be sufficient, presenting him with two options. More importantly, you provide a recommended approach. You share your POV.

 TALK TRACKS:

Negotiating Trade-Offs

➢ **Option 1:** To get this into production before the summit, there will be many moving parts, data loads, and testing required in a short amount of time. I can probably get this done if you pull in a team member to help with the testing and data prep. (The trade-off you're asking for is more resources.)

➢ **Option 2:** Instead of fully deploying this, I can have this ready to demo at the summit, including providing screenshots for marketing materials. This approach will allow us time to work through the data, complete the testing, and provide wiggle room for any gotchas. I recommend this plan as there's less risk, yet it meets the objective of introducing the program at the event, and we don't have to stop progress on another project by stealing their resource. (The trade-off you're asking for is more time.)

Ka-boom! You've ensured your boss knows the ask was more significant than expected. You've provided options for trade-offs and, more importantly, articulated your POV by stating what you think is the best path forward. Your recommendation is sound, so Jamal agrees that the second option makes the most sense and lets you know he'll take point for setting expectations with the leadership team.

Phew! You have successfully avoided the Salesforce admin danger zone and dodged late-night and weekend work.

By the way, why stop there? You're on a roll! How about proposing another trade-off, as there is something important to *you* that will likely have to push.

 ## TALK TRACK:

A Bonus Trade-Off Related to Your Career Objectives

> ➤ I had planned a few hours tomorrow to wrap up a Trailhead module in preparation for our Service Cloud launch. Given this timeline, I will no longer be able to do that. Would you be willing to cover for me next week at the status meeting so I can complete my training?

You're nailing this! Plus, extra credit for vocalizing a career development priority.

After you have a chance to review Cameron's data file and are comfortable it's in good shape, you call her to let her know you'll be scheduling a walk-through on Monday to demo the functionality before sending the screenshots over. You still believe you'll likely finish well before that, but you've padded the bill and added time for all the elements in the estimate equation.

Before you hang up, Cameron asks for a favor. She's been thinking about an AppExchange app you mentioned that allows you to send a link in an email with a fillable form. She says it would be great to capture the partner responses and asks if there is any way you could include that?

For a moment, you feel obligated since you told her about this, but you resist your natural inclination to say yes. You remember that bringing up great ideas doesn't obligate you to deliver them immediately. Plus, you have already committed to a fair amount of work in a short time.

"I'd love to do that for you, but I think I'd be putting the timeline at risk. Instead, how about if I send you an example of a form we used in a different project so you can see the tool in action and start thinking about how we might incorporate it going forward. How does that sound?"

It's a win-win as Cameron's happy with that suggestion, and you've successfully avoided expanding the scope you've committed to delivering.

Bravo! You're rocking these techniques. You avoided committing to a timeline or even providing an estimate until you had all the information. You provided value by introducing the art of the possible while setting expectations that these weren't things you could immediately address. You clearly defined MVP requirements. You considered the estimate equation and padded the bill to communicate a more realistic turnaround time. You then negotiated trade-offs with your boss to ensure the high-priority request with the quick turn-around time was being done *instead of* work you'd committed to, not *in addition to* adding it to the top of your pile. When asked to squeeze in something beyond the agreed scope, you said no in a way that kept you from overcommitting but still gave your business partner immediate value.

Can you see how those actions gave you a little breathing room and preempted likely chaos? The value-o-meter is sky high and the chaos level is on the decline. Well done!

CHAPTER 13:

THINGS YOU CAN STOP TO MAKE THE CHAOS COUNT DROP

In order to thrive and be successful,
you have to be able to set boundaries.

—Oprah Winfrey

A key foundation within the Agile world is the concept of teams meeting regularly to reflect on how to be more effective. A good retrospective, as these meetings are called, includes a discussion of things that worked well and acknowledgment of the things that didn't work well, including activities that may need to be adjusted or stopped altogether. So far, we've discussed processes you can implement and techniques to keep the chaos at bay. In this chapter, we'll cover things you might want to *stop* doing, as they may be contributing to your busyness and overwhelm.

As I looked back on the scenarios that caused significant stress or extra effort for me over the years, several themes emerged that warrant a halt or at least consideration of a course correction. Being mindful of these can help you consider whether something is a good use of your Salesforce admin time and skillset and when to say when because it's okay for certain things to be good enough. You have agency in your role and more control over your time each day than you probably give yourself credit for.

The value you bring to your organization includes combining your platform knowledge with your understanding of both the business needs and your stakeholders' readiness to weigh in on prioritization for Salesforce projects and the appropriateness of any Salesforce solution. Your discernment can help with sequencing, ensuring you spend your precious admin hours on the activities that will give your company the best bang for its Salesforce buck. A few small adjustments in how you respond to requests, how you engage in solutioning, and what you respectfully decline to take on can yield more time for value-adding projects, less rework, and less stress in your role.

Stop Confusing a Question with a Command

"Can you have this done by EOD?"

"Can we get this deployed before the sales meeting?"

"What would it take to get Live Agent launched in conjunction with the press release next week?"

I'm guessing your stakeholders have posed similar questions. And I'm willing to bet you moved mountains to make it happen. Here's what I implore you to take to heart, as this tip alone will give you hours of your life back. These are *questions*, not commands. They warrant consideration, conversation, and maybe a discussion about...you guessed it, trade-offs! They do not require you to drop everything and bust out the work without further clarification.

Let's pick one of the above examples and play this out.

"Can we get this deployed before the sales meeting?"

Scenario 1: Let's assume it really is an easy-breezy request, and you've got plenty of time to address it. "You bet! Unless we hit an unexpected gotcha, that should be no problem." (It never hurts to add this caveat to remind folks that both technology and data are prone to complexities.)

Scenario 2: You've already got a full plate of things you've committed to doing during this time. You can absolutely get it done, assuming you agree to a trade-off: "It's feasible, but there are several other things I agreed I would complete by then. One or more will have to be pushed out to meet that timeline. Can we review the list and get aligned on priorities?"

The conversation would be slightly different if your commitments weren't all for the same stakeholder. In that case, you might ask for help articulating the importance of completing the project in time for the meeting or the potential impact of not getting it done in time. Then you might say you'd like to consult your boss or the governance committee to explore if and how you should reshuffle your priorities.

Scenario 3: The request is significant. It will need substantial work to get it built and considerable testing before you'll be comfortable pushing it into production. You take a deep breath and answer: "Given that it's already Wednesday, even if I had a clear calendar and an army of Salesforce resources, there's no way we could implement this amount of change in that timeline without incurring risk and disruption."

Wait for it. The wrath is coming, right?

"Okay. That makes sense. I figured it couldn't hurt to ask."

More often than you may think, this is how it will play out. Granted, this stakeholder could have said that your answer was unacceptable, insisting that you do it no matter what. If it is an unreasonable or risky request, see the chapter on throwing the flag, as it would qualify as something to escalate. Most of the time, your stakeholders are legitimately inquiring about feasibility. The question is a jumping-off point for a discussion, not a command for you to jump. If there's a way to make it happen by bringing in additional resources, making different trade-offs, or deploying some but not all of it, you can get creative and collaborate on a solution. The key is getting used to hearing these asks and responding to them as questions, not commands.

When you take time to engage in conversation, you'll often find the person inquiring was simply curious or looking for information with no expectation that you would take any action. Maybe your CEO read an article about Live Chat over lunch and started to wonder what would be involved with adding that to the website at some future point in time. Maybe your sales leader heard a keynote about incorporating AI in the prospecting process and was curious whether this was an option. Before you roll up your sleeves and start doing copious amounts of research or planning a project just because they asked a question, clarify the question's intent and whether or not there is a desire for you to spend time addressing it.

TALK TRACKS:

Clarifying Intent Before Taking Action

➢ I'd have to do some research before I could answer that. Is this something you'd like me to prioritize?

➢ I'd need to spend a few hours determining what would be involved to make that happen. Would you like me to move forward? If so, can you please provide some additional context?

➢ I'm curious what prompted that question? It'll take me a little time to provide an answer, so before diving in, I'd like to understand the level of information you need and where it fits on the priority list.

There's a related topic regarding the acronym ASAP in a request. It's easy to receive it as a drop-everything-and-get-it-done directive, so I encourage you to consider this in the same vein as the questions above. It warrants conversation, clarification, and maybe trade-offs, but it doesn't necessarily mean you need to pull an all-nighter with no questions asked. Train your brain to hear ASAP differently, keeping in mind that it means only "as soon as possible," even when it's in all caps.

"This data needs to be loaded ASAP!"

Remember what I told you earlier about putting on your hat and getting to the heart of business requirements? That applies here, too. Don't make assumptions. Ask for clarification until you understand the urgency and implications of having it done or not done in a given time frame. This is one of those times when your reputation for being responsive and helpful will greatly benefit you. Your stakeholders will trust that you'd be all over it if it were easy and you were available. They'll trust that you aren't asking the questions just to throw up blockers or excuses but to legitimately explore impacts so you can determine how to prioritize for the greatest good.

 ## TALK TRACKS:

Uncovering What ASAP Means

➤ When precisely does this need to be completed?

➤ What is driving that timeline?

➤ Is this a critical step needed to complete other actions by a certain date? If so, what are those downstream activities?

➤ What's the implication of not having this completed by that deadline?

Once you have some context, answer the question by addressing their literal request, sharing the soonest possible time you could have it done given the size of the ask and your current constraints. For instance, "Based on what I've already got scheduled, the soonest I can get this done without impacting existing commitments is tomorrow afternoon. How does that sound?" If it sounds good, which will often be the case, you are golden. If not, this is where your questions to understand impact and discussions about trade-offs come into play.

Pro tip: Salesforce is a mission-critical business system in many organizations. There will be times when something does require urgent attention. Stuff breaks. Data gets corrupted. Unintended consequences sometimes occur with system changes. When this happens, communicate with your stakeholders the impact and the effort it will take to resolve: "We can get this done by morning, but it will likely mean a few team members will have a very late night to get it ready for production. Is this that urgent?" More often than not, even legitimately urgent issues aren't so pressing once your stakeholders understand what they might mean for the team.

Stop Providing Solutions if the Juice isn't Worth the Squeeze

"Can Salesforce [insert crazy idea here]?"

This question will be familiar to most Salesforce admins. On any given day, someone likely asks about the feasibility of something they want to accomplish. Can Salesforce do it? Given the platform's power and flexibility, and assuming there are no time or money constraints, the odds are good that the answer is yes.

But *should* Salesforce do it is an entirely different question that your inner product manager should raise. Any seasoned Salesforce professional has real-world examples of things they built that seemed like great ideas but that, in hindsight, ended up being more trouble than they were worth.

I'd love to hear your horror stories about things you wish you'd never agreed to do. Argh! I've got plenty of them! I once had the brilliant idea of creating a custom object to track our sales comp structure since it was so unusual that no off-the-shelf solutions could accommodate it. While it seemed like a good idea at the time, our comp plans changed so dramatically that I spent weeks every January redesigning the object from the ground up in addition to all the beginning-of-the-year Sales Ops fun. I suggested that we perhaps retire it given the required effort, but the genie was out of the bottle and no one would hear of not having it, so instead, January was a very rough month for me.

A sign of a good product manager is their ability to ensure that the right problems get addressed with the right-sized solutions. When you wear your product manager hat, this means not wasting time on things that don't matter and not overcomplicating your solutions. In the movie *Jurassic Park,* Jeff Goldblum's character says that just because you can clone a dinosaur doesn't make it a good idea. Some Salesforce admins I know have adopted the phrase "Don't clone dinosaurs" as a reminder to be deterministic about which problems they solve using the Salesforce platform and how they design solutions. A Salesforce professional recently heard me use this phrase and thought it was a warning against automating broken or outdated processes, an equally appropriate caution.

Understanding that just because you *can* do something doesn't mean you *should* is critical to not spending time on tasks that don't matter and optimizing the solutions you undertake. The trick is to figure out in advance when the work you're doing may fall into the cloning dinosaurs category. If we look at our stories collectively, common traits would likely emerge as leading indicators. There's no exact recipe to uncover when you're at risk of doing that, but your answers to these questions may trigger a flashing warning light to consider whether your work is warranted:

- Does the work benefit many and have lots of utility, or does it address a narrow, point-in-time problem? Yes, you could build a knocked-out custom object for that thing they are doing this week, but is it the best use of your time?

- Are you prepared for the amount of ongoing support it will require?

- Are you building something already available out of the box? Is there a more straightforward path that would provide almost as much benefit?

- Are you over-engineering to support a very rare edge case? Suppose you have a scenario that happens very infrequently. Could you set up something simple like an email alert to a business user who can manually address the issue instead?

- Is the solution pushing the limits of the platform or adding too much risk?

For each of these scenarios, it's likely the level of effort isn't proportional to the amount of value created or doesn't justify the opportunity cost. The juice isn't worth the squeeze. Sometimes requests will come your way to stand things up in Salesforce that probably don't belong there. If you can help a team understand why their proposed solution isn't a fit for Salesforce and save wasted effort, that's also a value add.

Configuration Caveats

Let's explore what cloning dinosaurs means in terms of designing Salesforce solutions. A rule of thumb is to follow the path of least resistance. A simple, declarative, no-code option is always where you should start. This is an easy rule for most Salesforce admins because it's generally all we do. Complexity doesn't just equate to code, however. Point and click can yield plenty of bloat and overkill. We can all share horror stories we encountered when getting under the hood in a new org. In hindsight, most of us can probably confess to deploying all sorts of things that deserved much more discussion before we flipped the proverbial switch.

The list below provides examples that deserve extra consideration. Remember, none of these things are inherently wrong. I'm not saying you should never include these as part of a Salesforce solution. Proceed cautiously and consider the implications, including the time it will take you to support these and the amount of confusion or complexity they may introduce into your org.

Examples of "Think Twice" Functionality

✓ Multi-select picklists, the Quick Create button, person accounts, and numerous other out-of-the-box features that can cause more trouble than they're worth.

✓ Anything that requires activating an org setting that can't be turned off once you enable it or introduces permanent changes in the org. Examples include custom fiscal years and divisions.

✓ Multi-Currency. (Hint: make sure you have a process for maintaining the exchange rate.)

✓ Renaming standard objects. While this may seem like a good idea, it will preclude you from using any out-of-the-box training materials. Plus, even when you change the labels, there are still places "under the hood" that reference the objects by their standard names, which can cause great confusion for admins and developers.

✓ Renaming field labels when using custom report types. This is another one that seems like a good idea until you realize there's no way to track which labels were changed, which inevitably means a future Salesforce admin in your org will wrack their brain trying to figure out what field they're looking at in the report. Plus, it's not a great user experience to drill through a report and not be able to find a field with that name on the record page.

Can you see how being intentional about what work you agree to take on and how you design solutions can save time and avoid future chaos? Can you think of any Salesforce solutions that, in retrospect, you would reconsider or at least revisit in terms of your approach?

Stop Automating Processes That Aren't Ready for Prime Time

Salesforce is not a business process in and of itself. It is a tool that enables and automates business processes. If someone cannot walk you through how a business process should work from end to end, they aren't ready for you. Or, as I like to say, if they can't put it on a whiteboard, you can't put it in Salesforce.

Hear me out. I'm not saying that value-adding Salesforce admins shouldn't shape business requirements or partner with stakeholders to design solutions. After all, we aren't order takers. We've established that we wear a BA hat and can help define and address process gaps. But because time is our most precious asset, we need to get involved *after* our business partners have done the work to define their business processes.

Refraining from automating processes that aren't fully baked doesn't mean your stakeholders must come prepared to address every minute detail required to set up a flow, trigger an email, or add entry criteria to an approval process. These are the nitty-gritty decisions your peeps likely won't have considered yet, and nor would you expect that. You'll work through that level of detail together as you start designing the solution, or at the very least, you'll provide them with a list of specific questions they need to answer for you to complete your work.

When you are engaged to assist with a Salesforce solution, your business partner should be able to answer a journalist's briefing: who, what, when, where, and why. Let's say your stakeholders want your help implementing a new program to provide discounted services for current customers. Great! Which customers are eligible? Which services are available for discount? Are there limitations on how many services a customer can get at a discounted rate? How long will this program last?

I already hear the naysayers. Those details don't matter and will get worked out later. Yes, but if Sales and Marketing haven't agreed on the basics and are still hashing out the program's framework, they probably aren't ready for your handiwork. By all means, conduct an initial consult, provide guidance on the type of information you'll need to engage, and then get on with your day. It's not that you don't want to be helpful or be at the table for critical operations discussions and decisions, but you have limited hours and significant value that you need to deliver. Sitting in unnecessary meetings has direct opportunity costs, not to mention the high risk of rework if you start solutioning something that isn't ready for prime time.

I've worked with people in many start-ups and companies in various states of flux who wanted Salesforce to automate business processes that were still half-baked. Generally speaking, those meetings went something like this:

Me: Which team will be responsible for entering that data?

Them: Blank stare.

Me: What are the steps for routing the approval?

Them: Lengthy discussion of various points of view, with no clear process for making these decisions.

Me: What should happen after that request is submitted? Are there additional teams that need to know about it?

Them: Blank stare. "Now that you mention it, I wonder if we'll need Legal to sign off. We haven't talked to them yet. We probably should."

You get the picture. The business team still needs to hammer out its process. At a bare minimum, they need to have enough clarity to walk you through the process from start to finish. Otherwise, you are burning hours that you need for all your day-job activities and value-adding projects. Ideally, if time permits, you can partner with them to document a business process flow and point out gaps that they need to flesh out before you can engage. Be as specific as possible regarding the questions you need them to answer and encourage them to reach out to you when they're ready.

Pro tip: Learn to create flowcharts and diagrams in Visio or Lucidchart. Walking your stakeholders through a business flow and noting significant gaps and empty boxes representing information you need is an excellent way to add value.

CAUTION! A CALM-THE-CHAOS CAVEAT

There is a difference between defining a business process at the highest level and defining functional or system requirements. If you hear that they will meet to "discuss requirements," get in on that meeting. Hearing their requirements firsthand allows you to ask questions and understand the desired outcome so you can ultimately deliver precisely what they need. You can provide context about the technical complexity and help differentiate between must-haves and nice-to-haves. Plus, you can add value as they walk through their ideal state by suggesting things they might not think to ask for and get ideas for so-called bonus features you might include.

Stop Over-Delivering. Be Intentional About What's Good Enough

Not only are most of us Salesforce folks people pleasers, but I'd bet most of us err on the side of being perfectionists. Unfortunately, this means we may spend more time than we need to on a particular task or pay too much attention to something that doesn't add a comparable amount of value. Perfectionism prevents us from getting to the important stuff.

With all your competing priorities, you can start making conscious decisions that something is good enough. One way to do this is to consider the Pareto principle, often called the 80/20 rule. In its most simple terms, this economic theory suggests that 80 percent of the value you provide will come from 20 percent of the work you do, and 80 percent of the work you do will result in only 20 percent of the value you provide. This means you want to be intentional about figuring out which efforts will give you the biggest bang for your buck. Applying the 80/20 rule can be a handy way to prioritize your time and help you consider when to stop working on something that may not be your highest-value action item.

The 80/20 rule can help you accept that incremental improvement can suffice and that the extra effort to make something perfect may not be worth it. Take data quality, for instance. Many of us who scrub data and manage databases for a living have a little Virgo in us. We like our data neat and tidy, without a hair out of place. As a Salesforce admin, you can do many things to improve data quality. From implementing dupe-blocker tools to adding validation rules to creating data quality exception reports and dashboards, dirty data has nothing on you!

That said, despite your best efforts, on any given day, fields will be blank, records will be wonky, and some errant user or integration will wreak havoc on your tidy database. It's par for the course. Solve the big problems impacting critical fields and records. Fix the root causes. Keep an eye out for new issues and proactively monitor things that matter, but don't take it upon yourself to scrub every field in every record. While they may make you crazy, ignore the data issues that aren't impactful and recognize that time spent cleaning non-essential data detracts from initiatives that will move the needle.

Knowing when to say when isn't always obvious. Here are examples of when you may be expending effort that isn't delivering the value proportionate to your time and the opportunity cost of other tasks you could be doing. As you read these, consider your open items and in-flight initiatives. What's not finished but probably should be if you were to acknowledge that it's good enough in its current state?

- You've built a knocked-out dashboard but can't get that one widget working quite the way you envisioned it, and you spend two more hours tinkering with that component. Stop working, share what you've built with your business partner, and see if it's sufficient.

- You are creating a presentation for a group of users who have asked you to share Salesforce tips and tricks. You've covered all the key topics, but the slides don't have quite the pizazz you'd like. Who cares? Those users will not remember you had a knocked-out PowerPoint with stunning animation. You don't need to spend hours making a perfect slide deck. Your expertise and your interaction with the users are what matter.

- You're reviewing the Salesforce Optimizer app to identify areas where you can shore up the system. You've worked through all the items that indicated potential risk or system issues, but there's still a long list of defunct infrastructure. I am a huge proponent of retiring technical debt, but you can work on non-essential cleanup incrementally. It shouldn't prevent you from focusing on projects that deliver immediate value to your stakeholders.

- You're deep in the weeds learning some new platform functionality you think might benefit your organization. To assess feasibility and fit, you don't yet need to know every nuance or exactly how things work. Spend enough time to understand the art of the possible and punt on the hands-on learning until you need to know.

Stop When You Care More Than They Do

Let's say you have a friend who tells you she would like to host a dinner party. She says her apartment is too small to fit everyone comfortably, so she asks if you'd mind having the party at your house, where there's much more room. "I'll take care of the details," she promises. "I'll handle the invitations, plan the menu, prepare the meal with you, and all you have to do is host."

Sure. Seems easy enough. She sends the invitations, so you are officially on the hook, but your friend goes radio silent as the date approaches. You call to ask her how many people have RSVPed and find out what's on the menu. You get a quick text: "Slammed. Will call 2nite." She continues to be missing in action, except for a quick call when she says, "I'm so sorry I got buried at work, so I haven't had a chance to think about this. Whatever you'd like to serve is fine with me." Suddenly, you're knee-deep in menu planning, house cleaning, and cooking to host *her* dinner party.

What in the world does this story have to do with Salesforce? If you don't recognize this behavior yet, trust me, you'll eventually experience stakeholder apathy and a bit of passing the buck. Your business process owner initiates a project for enhancements or net-new functionality and then suddenly goes silent, or at least is much less engaged than you need them to be. This tends to happen more when the Salesforce admin was previously part of the operational ranks, perhaps part of Sales Ops before stepping into the Salesforce admin role. Because you know what's needed, you pick up the slack. And guess what, they know you will! Before you know it, you find yourself scheduling the meetings, driving business process discussions, and knowing more about their new business process than they do.

Here are some red flags:

- They repeatedly cancel or reschedule meetings but aren't open to pushing back the timeline

- They contact you right before a meeting to say they can't make it and ask if you can please facilitate

- If there are any questions about the details of what you are building for them, they throw the question to you because they don't know the answer

- They respond to your request for decision points with "Whatever you think is fine with me."

To be clear, I'm not talking about making simple changes. For example, if your senior sales leader asks you to create a new field and add it to all the existing reports on the dashboard, and you've confirmed through conversation that it's the right approach, they should be able to get on with their day. You know what's needed and can knock it out without further direction. I'm also aware that many people in Salesforce admin roles are business process owners, perhaps key members of the RevOps or Customer Service team. In that instance, you may very well have a responsibility to own and execute all facets of the project accordingly, so own it and do it with gusto.

As I'm defining it here, stakeholder apathy is specific to business process owners who request net-new functionality or significant enhancements but don't follow through with ownership and initiative to ensure successful deployment and adoption. When faced with this dilemma, stepping in to carry the ball may seem like the proactive thing to do. Unfortunately, it typically takes more time than it should, putting you at risk of missing a deadline and stealing time you need to design, build, and test the right Salesforce solution. This also means you don't have a business partner to champion the change or partner with you on the rollout.

Stakeholder apathy is how functionality gets deployed but never adopted. It's how you never get out of the weeds after deploying certain functionality because you are the sole resident expert. When you find yourself carrying the torch on their behalf, it's another reason to remember that just because you *can* doesn't mean you *should*.

What can you do if you sense this is happening, or, better yet, how can you prevent it from happening in the first place? If the initiative is large enough, consider developing a mutual plan with built-in checkpoints and commitments you can point to if your business partner is missing milestones. Include steps to ensure they comprehend the solution and have some skin in the game. For instance, when your solution is getting close to the finish line, agree that your stakeholder will take point for presenting the functionality instead of you doing all the demos. Or, perhaps you are responsible for preparing the training materials and training users. You can agree in advance that your business partner, or their delegate, will do a "teach-back" where they walk through the materials as if they were teaching you, ensuring that someone on their team knows the material and understands the process as well as you do.

Suppose it's clear they aren't fulfilling their part of the bargain. In that case, have a candid conversation or recommend postponing the project until they have more time to devote to it or can assign a delegate. If you try that and still aren't getting what you need, throw the flag. Don't go it alone.

CHAPTER 14:

TO THINE OWN SELF BE TRUE

*We need to do a better job of putting ourselves
higher on our own "to-do" list.*

—Michelle Obama

The amount of change on the Salesforce platform means continual learning. Going above and beyond is hard work. Enjoying and profiting from your Salesforce journey for the long haul takes energy and enthusiasm. You can add value only when you can show up to work healthy, enthused, motivated, and ready to contribute. Leveraging processes and establishing business boundaries will go a long way toward calming the chaos, but prioritizing your mental and physical health must be part of the equation. Mental and physical well-being is a non-negotiable dependency for a successful Salesforce admin.

Burnout Is Real and Personal Heroics Are Not Sustainable

The World Health Organization (WHO) recently included burnout in its International Classification of Diseases, which has increased awareness, treatment options, and insurance coverage for work-related stress.[8] In other words, all you overachievers out there, this is a real thing you need to take seriously.

In the 2020/2021 Mason Frank Salary Survey, for the first time, the survey included a question for Salesforce professionals about whether they had experienced burnout in their current role, defined as follows: "Burnout is defined by exhaustion, cynicism, and inefficacy, or the stress that's generated by being in a constant state of busyness, feeling that no amount of effort is ever good enough." Of the respondents, 23 percent reported that they had experienced burnout once and 37 percent responded that they had more than once.[9]

Ironically, Salesforce professionals may be at a higher risk of burnout due to the job demands and because we are so passionate about our profession. The *Harvard Business Review* recently published an article called "When Passion Leads to Burnout."[10] The author addresses the fallacy in the oft-repeated phrase that if you do what you love, you'll never work a day in your life. They cite several studies claiming that people doing work they love and feel passionate about are at increased risk for burnout. One of the risk factors includes identifying so strongly with work that you lack balance between your work and personal life.

Yep, many of the enthusiastic, high-performing Salesforce admins I know would have to check that box.

Let's face it, most of us are Salesforce fanatics. We sport Ohana tattoos, name our dogs Astro, and dream of Golden Hoodies. Yet, there's always so much more we want to do and learn. Meet-ups and certifications and MVP aspirations, oh my! As if our day jobs aren't busy enough, there's an endless list of networking, training, and other activities that will advance our careers and provide us with the sense of community so unique to Salesforce. The key is to remember that it's a journey, not a sprint. You must build in time to take care of yourself.

A Real-Life Example

I once took on a grueling task of decommissioning a complex legacy system used by our sales team to request sales support and route deal approvals. It was a big project that I agreed to manage in addition to my day job. A trade-off would have served me well, so my first mistake was not insisting on additional resources or reducing the scope of my daily activities. I was already exhausted, and then right before going live, I came down with a gnarly bronchial infection, but I kept going. When laryngitis set in, I didn't stop working. I continued to facilitate training calls and meetings despite my hoarseness. I kept going until I couldn't anymore.

We decommissioned the old system and transitioned the functionality to Salesforce. It was a great success on paper, but for me personally, it was a disaster. My voice entirely vanished for weeks; not a single sound would come out. Even worse than the involuntary speaking hiatus, which those who know me can imagine was difficult, I lost the will to do anything related to that project and then anything at all work-related. The cumulative effect of my not taking enough downtime, not throwing the flag when I needed more resources, and not saying no when I was literally unable to speak wore me down. I ended up quitting that job, and it took me several months of time off to feel better and get my enthusiasm back. To this day, my voice hasn't fully recovered.

Five Critical Principles

Here's the thing. No matter how good your boss or employer's intentions are, no one but you can take responsibility for protecting your physical and mental health. These are not optional concerns you can skip over because you're busy and have a big project you need to get across the finish line. Stress builds up. Years of unhealthy eating and no exercise will catch up with you. A lack of sleep will wear you down. By no means can I proclaim that this is my area of expertise. Quite the opposite; I've been on the brink of burnout several times throughout my career. I admit I haven't entirely nailed this yet, but as I've learned to incorporate many of the tools and techniques discussed here, the external chaos has been dramatically reduced. I've recognized that much of what's remaining are things in my control.

I follow sites like Thrive Global and Calm so my LinkedIn and Twitter feeds force me to see articles about reducing stress and staying healthy instead of all work topics. I encourage you to use a sit-stand desk, meditate, drink a lot of water, practice yoga, or do whatever works for you to improve your physical and mental health. To that end, please consider the following five principles as essential to your successful Salesforce career as the other topics we covered.

There Will Always Be More To Do

We discussed the importance of an ownership mentality, but it has a downside to guard against. You will have endless improvement ideas. The list of things you want to add or change to improve your system and processes will be a mile long. For your well-being, get comfortable that there will always be more to do. As the saying goes, the work will always be there. You will never get to the bottom of the list. Good! Consider it job security. Write down your ideas and outstanding action items. Put them in your backlog. They will be there tomorrow. Then unplug and check out at a reasonable hour at the end of the day.

Recognizing that there will always be more to do also applies to your pursuit of certifications, badges, and whatever personal goals you set for yourself as part of your Salesforce journey. If you're in it for the long haul, the real value is getting the experience, not just checking the box. Remember, it's a marathon, not a sprint, and pace yourself.

 Pro tip: Start tracking how many hours you work each week. Be honest with yourself if you are logging in on weekends and evenings. Paying attention to this will remind you to stop at a reasonable hour. If the number is more significant than it should be, set a goal and track your progress toward hitting it.

Vacations Are Not Optional

According to the U.S. Travel Association, half of all American workers didn't use all their vacation days in 2018.[11] Even during the pandemic in 2020, employees worked harder and took less time off despite the stress we were all feeling.[12] I have to confess that I did not use all of my vacation time then, and, in fact, I rarely ever have. I'm sharing this with you to hold myself accountable. As long as I'm gainfully employed, I'm taking off every darn vacation day I get, and I hope you'll do the same. Paid time off is part of your compensation package. You wouldn't give back part of your salary, so why would you work more than you need to?

You do not need to apologize for taking time off, even when it's seemingly inconvenient because of workload or project deadlines. Instead, share your plans with as much advance notice as possible, and provide colleagues an ample heads-up so they aren't counting on you while you're gone. If it helps you think about it any differently, time off is a critical ingredient to allow you to rest and recharge to continue delivering great work for your constituents.

 Pro tip: If you don't have a significant vacation planned and risk not using all your time off, consider scheduling a few half days and long weekends to give yourself some downtime.

Don't Get Hung Up on Mistakes

Stuff happens. As a Salesforce admin, you juggle many balls and make Salesforce magic possible. But you're also human, so you sometimes make mistakes. Don't beat yourself up or dwell on it. Instead, determine who needs to know and communicate as directly and swiftly as possible. Figure out what you can learn from the experience and how to prevent it from happening again. Write down your lessons learned. Determine how to get a resolution, and then make sure you do. Most importantly, let it go; get over it.

After a colossal screw-up that I just couldn't get over early in my career, my boss at the time gave me some great perspective: "Since 98 percent of what you do each day is hitting it out of the ballpark, even with said screw-up, I'm still coming out way ahead in this exchange." Consider all the wins you put on the board daily and remember this advice when you need to move on after a mistake.

Put Your Hand Down if You Feel Like It

One of the best things I learned from my time as an independent consultant was the practice of placing a dollar value on my time. It was easy to stay focused on the work my clients hired me for, as I couldn't bill for anything else. Consultants get paid only for work in scope, so that's all they do. On the other hand, employees are often encouraged to take on various activities outside the scope of their day job.

Once you establish your reputation as a high performer, you will likely be tagged for special projects and cross-functional initiatives. I'm referring to things like the Culture Committee, the New Intern Welcome Program, the Office Ergonomics Improvement Team, or the Happy Hour Planning Committee. Do these sound familiar? If any of them are part of your job description, or perhaps the pet project of your boss, then consider them to be in scope and do them well. If you enjoy these pursuits and they contribute to your work satisfaction, by all means, keep doing them. If participating gives you a leadership opportunity that you've been seeking or a chance to grow relationships and network with leaders at your firm, jump in.

If you do not personally get value from these activities, you do not need to feel obligated. Just as with stakeholders, there are ways to say no and politely opt out. Thank them for asking you. Explain that you would love to participate but have an exceptionally full plate right now. If you struggle with saying no, see if there's something small you can take on without a more significant commitment. For instance, "Unfortunately, I don't have time to participate fully right now, but I'm happy to assist if you need extra hands to help set up before the event."

You get to control the pace of your career. You choose when you want to hustle and when you actively seek greater responsibilities. You also get to decide when you lean out. That doesn't mean you stop showing up and adding value; it means you can determine your willingness to take on something outside your scope.

When you're nailing it on the Salesforce front, making fans across the organization, and continually putting wins on the board, your boss or management team won't remember or care that you opted to skip non-essential duties.

Lean into the Ohana

Throughout this book, I've mentioned that you don't have to go it alone. Thanks to the Salesforce Ohana, the highly engaged, wonderfully supportive Salesforce community, it's true. Get involved online or in person and take full advantage of all the Ohana offers in terms of learning, career advice, and the personal and professional relationships you can form. Join user groups, attend regional Salesforce meetups, and participate in online study sessions. Not only will you connect with great folks and learn like crazy, but hearing about what other companies are doing will give you fantastic ideas and insight. Knowledge sharing is the way to accelerate your Salesforce experience even if you haven't yet "been there, done that."

As beneficial as the Ohana can be, it can be intimidating and even discouraging if you compare yourself to others who are "ahead" of you on their Salesforce journey. Lean in and you'll get a ton out of it, but you can also lean out if it's not your thing. Beware the Ohana overwhelm. It's okay to use the Trailblazer community site as a resource without answering any questions yourself. SteveMo has you covered. (Salesforce MVP Steve Molis has responded to more than 82,000 questions on the Trailblazer Community site. If he hasn't answered one of your questions, the odds are good that he will!)

There's no requirement that you actively brand yourself as a Salesforce superstar if that's not part of your career objective. Instead, focus on knocking it out of the park for your stakeholders, teammates, and users. Too busy for a Salesforce Saturday? Stop feeling guilty. Not comfortable presenting at a Dreamin' event? No worries. It takes work to stay on top of your Salesforce game. Keeping up with your company or client initiatives to ensure that you can add value takes effort. It's okay if that's all you've got to give right now or if you want Salesforce to be your profession but not your hobby or friend network. Making companies wildly successful with Salesforce is what the Ohana is all about. Jump in when you are ready, take what you need, and participate on whatever terms work for you.

WRAP-UP

"Thank you" is the best prayer that anyone could say.
I say that one a lot.
Thank you expresses extreme gratitude, humility, understanding.

—Alice Walker

Congrats on finishing this book, and thank you for sharing your valuable time with me. I hope you enjoyed it. We covered a lot of ground! I hope you'll act on the things you learned here so you can enjoy the benefits of having a seat at the table with your business partners instead of working the window at McAdmin's Drive-Thru.

You possess high-demand Salesforce skills that people want and companies need. You have an extraordinary career opportunity. You get to help people every day, learn new things, and make great money while you do it. You're a rockstar. You make a difference. Own it.

On busy days, keep in mind that the fact that you have a to-do list a mile long is a testament to the value you bring. People want you on their projects. They trust that you'll show up and knock it out of the park, time after time. Breathe. Have fun. Be grateful. You get to do Salesforce for a living.

Remember to take care of yourself with the same level of attention you give your users, your database, and your dashboards. I wholeheartedly believe that those of us lucky enough to have this role should pay it forward by adding value to all aspects of the job. But do it on your terms, with processes and rules of engagement that work for you. After all, it's your acumen, energy, and creativity, not some Salesforce pixie dust, that make the magic happen.

Select one or two tips from this book and set a goal for implementing them. Perfect your questioning skills. Find opportunities to articulate your POV. Try out some talk tracks to see how they sound. Feel free to change them up so they sound like words you would say, as it's the concepts that count. Pause to consider the estimate equation the next time someone asks how long something will take. Practice asking for trade-offs. Recognize that having a calm-the-chaos strategy is as essential to your long-term Salesforce career journey as acquiring more Salesforce certifications.

Watch how your relationships with your stakeholders begin to change for the better. Observe how your Salesforce solutions improve. Note how much better it feels to solve problems proactively instead of continually fighting fires. Rinse and repeat.

You've got this!

QUICK FAVOR

First of all, your time is incredibly valuable, so thank you for reading my book! May I ask a quick favor?

Will you PLEASE take a moment and leave an honest review on Amazon?

Did something resonate with you? Was there an idea that really hit home? Is there something you'll implement right away? Even one or two sentences to share a key takeaway would be extremely helpful!

Reviews are the best way to help others find this book and decide if it could be useful for them.

PS) I would be incredibly grateful if you could help spread the word about this book online. Shoutouts and pictures with the book in hand would make my day and be much appreciated!

I'd also love to hear from you directly. Reach out at jodi@sfadminbook.com and visit www.sfadminbook.com for updates and related resources to help you rock your Salesforce role.

Thank you!

ACKNOWLEDGMENTS

I've had the pleasure to work with some of the best Salesforce talent in the business, including some extraordinary Salesforce admins and all-around great humans. From Andrew Smith, the very first Salesforce admin I hired 20-something years ago, to Megan Aldana and Mike Keyzer, whom I've had the pleasure of working with in several different companies, from Cora Thornton-Stocks and the rest of the fantastic IH crew and all the #Awesome Admins I've encountered along the way, thank you for all you've taught me. You were my role models when thinking about what it takes to be a remarkable Salesforce professional.

Randy Kish, thank you for serving as the wizard behind the curtain more times than I can count. It's been a great partnership, even as we learned many lessons in this book the hard way! Tani Long, your stellar training classes have produced so many rockstar admins that your name should be up in lights. Thank you both for reading the first draft and offering great feedback and the encouragement to keep going! I believe wholeheartedly that the best fun we'll all have in this fantastic Salesforce space is yet to come.

I had so many generous volunteers when I asked for beta readers, including Sam Roberts, Adam Ronhovde, Justin Melcarek, and Neha Modha. Your thoughtful feedback improved this book and, more importantly, gave me the confidence to release it to the world. Thank you for that!

I have to give a special shout-out to Dodi Friedenberg, who went so far above and beyond with editorial assistance and insightful commentary. The publishing world missed an opportunity to snag her, but the Salesforce ecosystem is all the better because of it—as is my book! Dodi, I cannot thank you enough!

To my rockin' promotion team who helped me get the word out—too numerous to name—thank you for your support, creativity, and energy!

I had no idea publishing this book would yield so many new friends across the globe with so much generous experience and enthusiasm to share.

The Salesforce Ohana is the real deal!

JH

ABOUT THE AUTHOR

Jodi Hrbek has spent two decades implementing and optimizing the Salesforce platform for fast-growing start-ups and enterprise organizations. She hired and managed over 25 Salesforce admins while in leadership roles on the Salesforce client-side and coached and advised dozens more during her four-year tenure at Salesforce and as an implementation consultant.

Jodi's mission is to turn good Salesforce teams into great ones, exponentially increasing the value companies realize from their Salesforce investment.

Her motto is "Work Smart. Hike Often," so when she's not doing something Salesforce-related, she's usually on a trail in the Texas Hill Country with one of her many rescue dogs.

You can find her online at www.jodihrbek.com or network with her at linkedin.com/in/jodihrbek.

ENDNOTES

1   "Salesforce Administrator Careers." *Trailhead*, Salesforce, https://trailhead.salesforce.com/career-path/admin.

2   Linkner, Josh. "Why Success Depends on Thinking Like an Owner." *Inc.*, 9 Aug. 2016.

3   "International Institute of Business Analysis™: IIBA®." *The Global Standard for Business Analysis | IIBA®*, https://www.iiba.org/career-resources/new-to-business-analysis/.

4   "Salesforce Business Analyst: Quick Look." *Trailhead*, Salesforce, https://trailhead.salesforce.com/en/content/learn/modules/salesforce-business-analyst-quick-look/learn-about-the-salesforce-business-analyst-role?trail_id=get-started-as-a-salesforce-business-analyst.

5   Altucher, James. "FAQ on How to Become an Idea Machine." *James Altucher*, 6 Jan. 2015, https://jamesaltucher.com/blog/faq-on-how-to-become-an-idea-machine/.

6   Salesforce. "Examples of Advanced Formula Fields / Formula Operators and Functions by Context." *Developer Portal*, Salesforce, https://developer.salesforce.com/docs/atlas.en-us.usefulFormulaFields.meta/usefulFormulaFields/customize_functions.htm.

7   "Examples of Advanced Formula Fields." *Help and Training Community*, Salesforce, https://help.salesforce.com/s/articleView?id=sf.useful_advanced_formulas.htm&type=5.

8   Chatterjee, Rhitu, and Carmel Wroth. "Who Redefines Burnout as a 'Syndrome' Linked to Chronic Stress at Work." *NPR*, NPR, 28 May 2019, https://www.npr.org/sections/health-shots/2019/05/28/727637944/who-redefines-burnout-as-a-syndrome-linked-to-chronic-stress-at-work.

9   *Mason Frank Salary Survey 2020-21*. Mason Frank International, www.masonfrank.com.

10 Moss, Jennifer. "When Passion Leads to Burnout." *Harvard Business Review*, 1 July 2019, https://hbr.org/2019/07/when-passion-leads-to-burnout.

11 Mcooper@ustravel.org. "Study: A Record 768 Million U.S. Vacation Days Went Unused in '18, Opportunity Cost in the Billions." *U.S. Travel Association*, 16 Aug. 2019, https://www.ustravel.org/press/study-record-768-million-us-vacation-days-went-unused-18-opportunity-cost-billions.

12 Jdickler. "The Year Is over and Workers Left Almost All of Their Vacation Days on the Table." *CNBC*, CNBC, 31 Dec. 2020, https://www.cnbc.com/2020/12/31/this-is-what-happens-to-all-those-vacation-days-that-never-got-used.html.